CW00522544

METALLICA

LEFT Shrouded by shadow, Cliff looks on to his bandmates during an early Metallica show, circa 1983.

THIS IS A CARLTON BOOK

Published in Great Britain in 2015 by
Carlton Books Limited
20 Mortimer Street
London W1T 3JW

Previously published as *Metallica: The Thrash Stash* in 2013

Copyright © 2015 Carlton Books Limited

A CIP catalogue for this book is available from the British Library.

ISBN 978-1-78097-617-4

Printed in China

10 9 8 7 6 5 4 3 2 1

METALLICA

THE STORY OF HEAVY METAL'S BIGGEST BAND

JERRY EWING

CARLTON
BOOKS

CONTENTS

RIGHT James Hetfield taking care of his burned arm before going on stage, summer 1992.

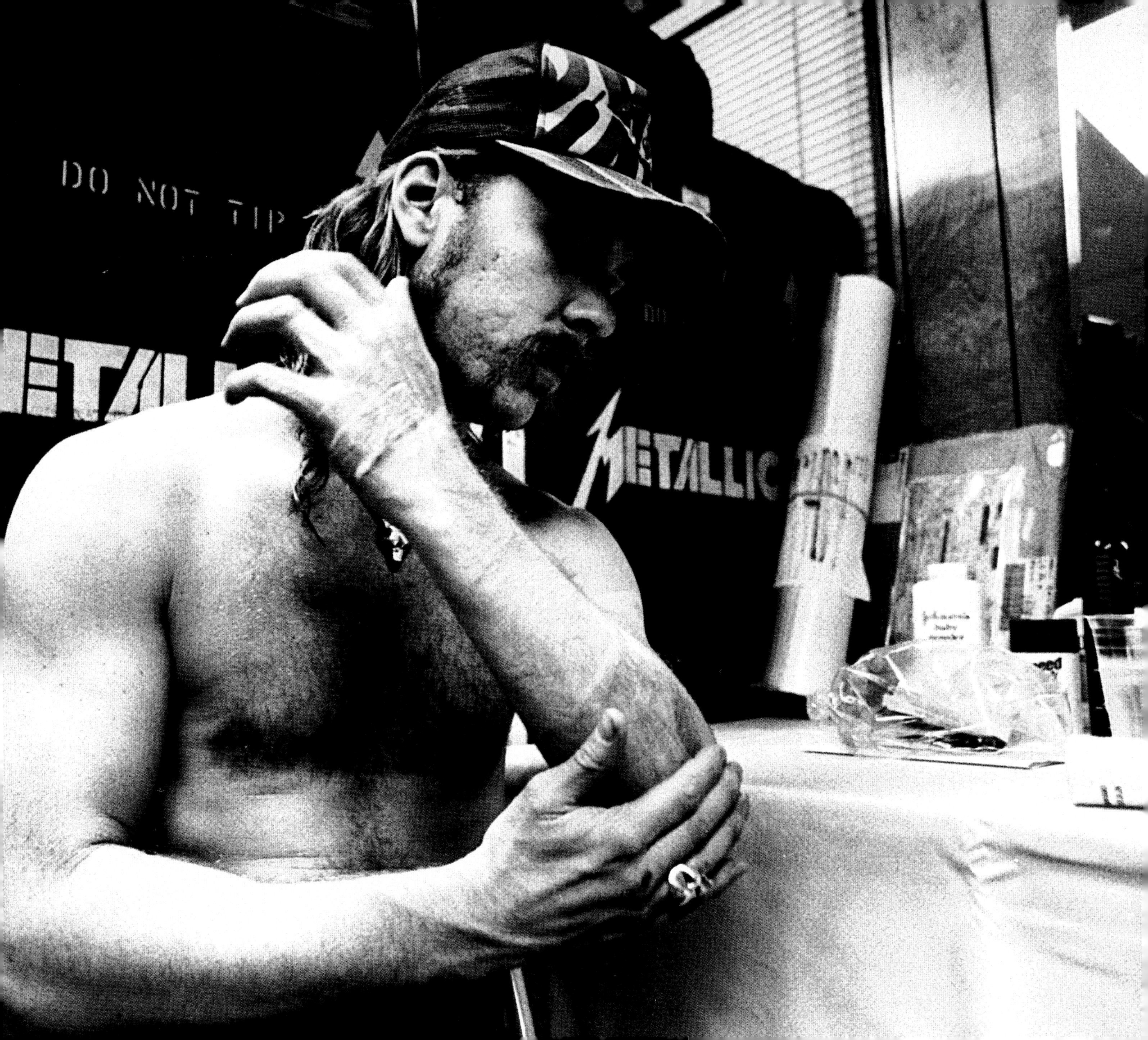
DO NOT TIP
METALLICA

INTRODUCTION

It's not often you get to see one of your favourite bands go from playing a club the size of the Marquee to a cavernous concert hall such as Wembley Arena in the space of 12 days. But then Metallica are no ordinary band. And much like their own unique tale, this is no ordinary story either.

In 1990 Metallica were still busying themselves working on their forthcoming 'Black Album'. They'd rounded off their epic Damaged Justice Tour in support of *...And Justice For All* on October 8, 1989, but by May of the next year were ready to go again. The European leg of that tour had seen the band play three nights at the Hammersmith Odeon. For the 1990 tour, the band's appeal and ambition (remember there was no new studio product on offer) saw them set to appear at Wembley Arena – at the time the largest arena venue London had to offer.

However, before they even made this giant stride in their career, there was something far more intimate to be had. Word had bandied around the London metal music press for a day or two that the band were planning something special to kick off their European jaunt. The morning of May 11, word came through to the *Metal Forces* offices (the magazine for which I was Deputy Editor at the time) that the band were planning to play a secret show as support to Seattle-based power metallers Metal Church, who were in town at the time. Billed as Vertigo (not The Frayed Ends as some sources suggest), the name of their then-UK record label might have been a bit of a giveaway, and indeed one had to feel a bit for Metal Church, a great band in their own right, as it didn't take long for word to hit the streets of London and everyone was clamouring for a ticket.

Fortunately we had contacts within Metallica's inner camp and a few sacred guest list places were secured. Arriving at a Marquee that was far more packed than I think I'd ever witnessed, the real giveaway for the hugely expectant crowd was an enormous white drum kit bearing two Danish flags. When Metallica hit the stage the place erupted. The gig itself passed in a blur of sweaty headbanging and ferociously great heavy metal that evoked memories of those 1984 Marquee gigs or that 1987 100 Club show! You knew you were witnessing something special.

Equally, just under two weeks later within Wembley's far more bland setting Metallica still strove to bring that club gig mentality to the bigger stage. They achieved it too, because of the kind of band they are. Metalheads playing for metal fans. It's a bond that whatever trials and tribulations that their later career might throw up, has never been broken.

Over two years later, as they strode unassailably towards the top of the heavy metal tree, Metallica once again played Wembley Arena. Two nights this time, and these shows included the famed Snakepit, another attempt to keep that link with their fans. My pass on one of those nights granted me access to said pit, and without hesitation I entered as the band struck up the opening bars of 'Enter Sandman'. I hadn't even considered the effect such close proximity to the on-stage pyro might be. A full 20 years down the line I think my eardrums have just about recovered!

JERRY EWING, LONDON

OVERLEAF Thirty years before – Burton, Ulrich, Hammett and Hetfield – a monster ready to be unleashed, 1982.

RIGHT Thirty years later – Hetfield, Hammet, Ulrich and Trujillo – some kind of monster indeed, 2011.

PLEASE
DO NOT
SIT ON
STEPS

THE EARLY YEARS

For many people, the birth of Metallica would centre around the now legendary advertisement placed in the Los Angeles-based classified newspaper *The Recycler* which simply read "Drummer looking for other metal musicians to jam with. Tygers Of Pan Tang, Diamond Head and Iron Maiden."

It was that ad that brought together Ulrich and James Hetfield for the very first time and months later the same ad (that Ulrich kept running) led to Dave Mustaine joining the band as well. But to get to the very earliest roots of Metallica you must look back to Copenhagen, Denmark in 1973.

To Copenhagen we go to discover the young Lars Ulrich's introduction to the world of heavy rock. Ulrich's father Torben was a Danish tennis professional. Indeed this was the career path it seemed that the youthful Lars would also take, and by the time he was 16, in 1979, Lars Ulrich moved with his family to Los Angeles to further his tennis training. And indeed we might never have heard of Metallica had not Ulrich senior received some passes for a Deep Purple concert at Copenhagen's KB Hallen back in February 1973, the very same venue where he was taking part in a tennis tournament. When a family friend announced he could not attend the concert, the nine-year-old Lars was handed what would prove to be a golden ticket.

Deep Purple, then on tour promoting their *Machine Head* album, simply astounded the young Ulrich with their dazzling and incendiary performance. From that moment he was hooked on heavy rock, purchasing his first Deep Purple album the next day. Within three years he would have his first drum kit. Suddenly there was a direct challenge to tennis in the life of Lars Ulrich.

In the meantime, in Downey, California, a suburb of Los Angeles, a young James Hetfield began taking piano lessons aged nine, which sparked an interest in music for the shy youngster. From this he developed a passion for popular heavy rock bands of the 1970s. Bands like Led Zeppelin, Thin Lizzy. AC/DC, Black Sabbath, Ted Nugent, Deep Purple, and above all, Aerosmith. He swiftly progressed from piano to playing his older half-brother David's drum kit, and by the time Hetfield was 14 he was playing guitar. He joined a band called Obsession that played cover songs by many of the bands he liked so much. After about a year and a half the band fell apart. Around this same time James went to live with his half-brother David in Brea, California after the death of his mother, who died of cancer after refusing medical treatment due to her Christian Scientist beliefs. While attending Brea Olinda High

LEFT The original lineup backstage at The Stone in San Francisco, September 18, 1982; (L to R) Mustaine, Ulrich, Hetfield and McGovney.

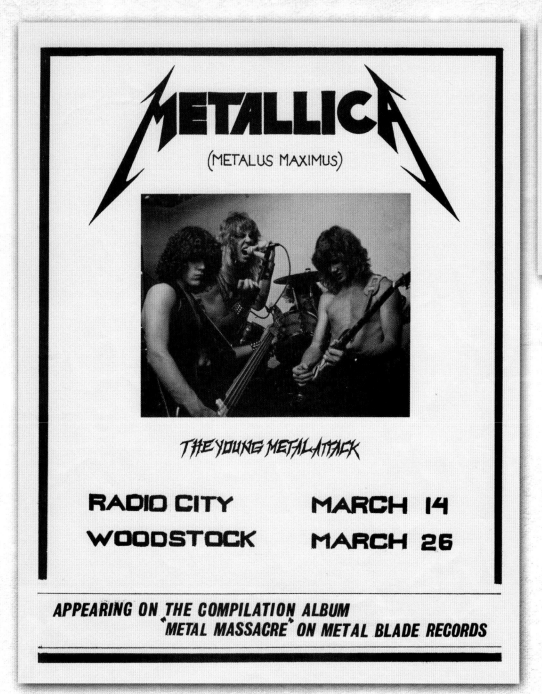

METALLICA

(METALUS MAXIMUS)

THE YOUNG METAL ATTACK

RADIO CITY   **MARCH 14**

WOODSTOCK   **MARCH 26**

APPEARING ON THE COMPILATION ALBUM
'METAL MASSACRE' ON METAL BLADE RECORDS

AMOUNT $ 100.00   No.

RECEIVED OF PETTY CASH

Whisky A-Go-Go 8/27/82

FOR Metallica

CHARGE TO B.O.

APPROVED BY   RECEIVED BY

FISCH STATY AND PRTG. CO. - (213) 742-0211

"THERE ARE A LOT OF SOAP OPERAS AND PETTY DRAMAS THAT COME FROM BEING IN THIS BAND." *Kirk*

ABOVE Flyer for the first two Metallica shows ever (although the March 26 show was eventually cancelled.)

ABOVE RIGHT Receipt for payment for a show at the Whisky a Go Go on August 27, 1982.

LEFT A rare shot of Mustaine and Hammett together at Cliff Burton's first gig with the band, March 5, 1983 at The Stone.

ABOVE Receipt for payment for a show at the Troubadour on August 2, 1982. Signed by Ron McGovney.

ABOVE Concert ticket for a show at the Troubadour on August 2, 1982.

RIGHT From the *Garage Days Re-Revisited* photo shoot, Germany 1987.

School James formed a band called Phantom Lord with Hugh Tanner, follwed by Leather Charm. Once again Hugh Tanner was there, along with Jim Mulligan – and a classmate called Ron McGovney.

McGovney had befriended James Hetfield at Downey High School in 1977, and stayed in touch when Hetfield moved to Brea in 1980. When Hetfield formed Leather Charm and needed a bass player he taught McGovney how play, and convinced him to join the band. Leather Charm never played any gigs but they did write three original songs called 'Hit The Lights', 'Handsome Ransom' and 'Let's Go Rock 'n' Roll'. The first became Metallica's debut song, while riffs of the other two would be combined on 'No Remorse'.

While this was going on, a 15-year old, fiercely independent Dave Mustaine from La Mesa, California, had escaped an overbearing Jehovah's Witness upbringing and was striking out on his own. He practiced earnestly on his beloved B.C. Rich electric guitar and in 1980

joined heavy metal band Panic. Disaster would strike after the quartet's first gig, when fellow guitarist Mike Leftwych and the band's sound engineer Joe were killed in a car accident. While in Panic, Mustaine did write some riffs that later ended up on Metallica and Megadeth tracks.

Meanwhile, further north in California, in Castro Valley, a youthful Cliff Burton was introduced to classical music by his father, and like James Hetfield, he too began taking piano lessons. His interest in music spread beyond classical to southern rock, country music, jazz, blues and eventually heavy metal. Tragedy struck the young Burton when his elder brother Scott, died of a cerebral aneurysm at the age of 16. Cliff, who had just taken up playing the bass guitar, announced to his parents "I'm going to be the best bassist for my brother". Often he practiced up to six hours a day. He formed the band EZ-Street with future Faith No More members Jim Martin and Mike Bordin, before the band morphed into Agents of Fortune. During this period Burton

developed his playing style, with an early version of his trademark bass solo that would end up on Metallica's debut album, and the well known bass intro to 'For Whom The Bell Tolls'.

Of course, none of this would really be of any importance, had not an 18-year old Lars Ulrich made his way over to London in 1981. Ulrich had purchased Diamond Head's now legendary 1980 *Lightning To The Nations* debut album and was enraptured with the band. He travelled to catch a show at the Woolwich Odeon, after which he managed to sneak backstage to meet his heroes. Ulrich having nowhere to stay, guitarist Brian Tatler invited him to crash at the floor of his Stourbridge home. And here, over the next two weeks, Ulrich had his eyes opened to the burgeoning NWOBHM (New Wave of British Heavy Metal) scene.

Ulrich travelled back to Los Angeles, and duly placed the aforementioned ad in *The Recycler*. James Hetfield answered that ad and as they say, the rest is history…

THRASH METAL & THE BAY AREA

There's absolutely no doubting that the 1980s was a massive decade for metal music. The advent of MTV in 1981 would give rise to all manner of hair metal acts, worthy or not, who made the most of record companies spending big bucks on promotional videos to get their hair-sprayed charges airtime in an attempt to sell more records.

This, of course, set in chain a series of events which led to the same record labels clamouring for like-minded acts to run through the same process until the already limpid thin talent pool was run dry. Hair metal arguably reached its apotheosis in 1987, when the likes of Bon Jovi, Motley Crue and Guns N' Roses and even Poison stood atop the rock world like colossi. Yet within the space of four short years, for many the hair metal bubble had burst.

While all this was going on, bubbling under the mainstream and snarling with an ever increasing rage – be it against preening glam rockers or, often far more pertinently, the establishment and social injustice, was another subgenre of heavy metal, which would come to be known as thrash metal. This was music that took its cues from the heavier moments of 1970s rock, Black Sabbath, Motörhead

and Judas Priest being prime examples, but also looked to the grittier new metal music that was made by the likes of Iron Maiden, Diamond Head, Raven, Angel Witch and especially Venom. The latter may have been viewed by and large by the metal establishment of the day as a bit of a joke, but for younger fans, clamouring for something new and even more exciting, the breakneck speed and sheer dynamic aggression that was offered up by Venom's 1981 debut album *Welcome To Hell* and its 1982 follow-up *Black Metal* were simply gold dust.

This was the kind of music that was inspiring the likes of the young Lars Ulrich and bands like Obsession and Leather Charm, who featured James Hetfield, EZ-Street featuring Cliff Burton and Panic featuring Dave Mustaine. And yet the sounds these bands were

ABOVE LEFT Early Bay Area thrash metal allies Laaz Rockit.

OPPOSITE Exodus with Hammett in the lineup, opening for Metallica at The Stone, San Francisco, March 5, 1983.

ABOVE Heathen, related to Metallica in more ways than one.

beginning to develop were not simply a pastiche of the NWOBHM. Typically, as with geographical shift came a sonic change as well. Seeking out aggressive forms of music in which to find inspiration, the young metal bands who were developing in America, notably in Southern California and later down in Florida as well, looked to UK punk acts like GBH, the Anti-Nowhere League and Discharge to lend a more frenetic and frantic edge to the sounds that they were creating.

While the sounds emanating from Florida took heaviness to extreme levels with bands like Obituary and the aptly named Death following the lead set by San Francisco's own Possessed in helping create the death metal genre, the latter were also a staple part of what became known as the Bay Area Scene, which for thrash metal would be the hub of early activity and a launch pad for the most influential and successful of all the thrash metal bands, namely Metallica.

The irony here, of course, is that Metallica were, in fact, from Los Angeles, and didn't hail from San Francisco at all. In fact it wasn't until the autumn of 1982, when Lars and James encountered the band Trauma, featuring Cliff Burton on bass at the Whisky a Go Go in West Hollywood that the wheels of the Bay Area Scene were truly set in motion. With original Metallica bassist Ron McGovney's position within the band under scrutiny (both James Hetfield and newly acquired lead guitarist Dave Mustaine felt McGovney did not contribute enough to the band), Burton's performance had seriously impressed the two main figures within the newly formed Metallica. So much so they asked him to join the band. Burton declined.

Metallica played their first ever gig in San Francisco at The Stone on September 18, 1982, which would have given the band a feel for the area. Already established was the venue Ruthie's Inn, a pro-punk and hardcore venue run by disillusioned jazzhead Wes Robinson, which was becoming increasingly pro-metal friendly. Other notable venues in the Bay Area were the Old Waldorf, both Keystones in Berkeley and Palo Alto, the Omni, the Kabuki Theater and the Warfield. Exodus, a thrash band who featured Kirk Hammett on guitar were one of the prime early movers of the thrash scene in the Bay Area.

Ron McGovney played his last gig with Metallica at San Francisco's Mabuhay Gardens on November 30, 1982. By December 10 he was no longer a member of the band. Instead, Cliff Burton finally accepted the offer to join Metallica, on the condition they moved to the Bay Area. This they duly did in February 1983, moving into a house on 3132 Carlson Boulevard in El Cerrito, rented by then Exodus manager Mark Whitaker. Metallica played their first ever gig with Cliff Burton at The Stone in San Francisco on March 5, 1983 with Exodus opening for them. From that day on, the Bay Area's status within the annals of heavy metal history was sealed.

During the following years the Bay Area scene flourished. The likes of Laaz Rockit, Exodus, Death Angel, Legacy, who later became Testament, Heathen, Forbidden (Evil) and Violence (who both featured Rob Flynn, later of Machine Head) all flourished as the thrash metal movement gained a momentum all its own, the intense tape-trading scene securing the bond between fans in a pre-internet era that helped to set thrash fans apart from their more commercially and MTV-minded adversaries.

True, only Metallica made the big time from this early season of hope, although notable mentions must be made of both Exodus, who really deserved a place in thrash's Big Four (when it came), Testament and Death Angel, and also to Rob Flynn, for taking the thrash model and reworking it in the 1990s to much success.

THE 1980s

After Lars Ulrich and James Hetfield met in May 1981 via Ulrich's ad in *The Recycler*, the two indeed jammed together, but Hetfield thought Ulrich couldn't play well enough and they went their separate ways. Then in October 1981, Lars approached James again, convincing him to join a band as he'd got a spot on a metal compilation being planned by his friend Brian Slagel – and Metallica was formed.

The band's first recording was a version of 'Hit The Lights', an old Leather Charm song, with Ulrich playing drums and Hetfield on bass, rhythm guitar and singing. It also featured two solos by guitarist Lloyd Grant. They appeared on the album called *Metal Massacre*, credited as Metallica, alongside the likes of Ratt, Bitch, Steeler and Cirith Ungol. For a second pressing they recorded a new version with Ron McGovney on bass and Dave Mustaine's solos.

The legendary *Power Metal* and *No Life 'Til Leather* demos followed. On the strength of the *No Life...* demo, Megaforce owner Jon Zazula signed the band and packed them off to tour the east coast and then on to Rochester, New York to record their debut album.

The proposed lineup for *Kill 'Em All* was Ulrich, Hetfield, Cliff Burton and Dave Mustaine. However the volatile Mustaine, under pressure from drink and substance issues that had damaged his relationship with the band, was sacked and sent back to California, where he would form Megadeth. Kirk Hammett, of old touring partners Exodus, replaced Mustaine, and it was this quartet who recorded *Kill 'Em All*. Released in July 1983, the album was not a financial success, but it did reach No. 120 on the *Billboard* album chart and sent shockwaves through the metal underground. The band toured with NWOBHM act Raven, and, having worked on demos for their second album, made their very first venture to Europe, supporting Venom on their Seven Dates of Hell Tour.

In February 1984, directly after the tour with Venom, Metallica entered Copenhagen's Sweet Silence studios to begin work on what would become their next album, *Ride The Lightning* with engineer and co-producer Flemming Rasmussen.

LEFT Death Angel, whose first demo tape was produced by Kirk Hammett.

BELOW Lars goofing around in San Francisco, spring 1987.

LEFT Flyer for the fourth ever
Metallica show, April 23, 1982.

ABOVE Early magazine ad for spring
1983 tour of the East Coast of the USA.

ABOVE Receipt for a bass guitar Cliff Burton bought
in San Francisco in October 1984.

"WE HAVE BULLETPROOF VESTS ON WHEN IT COMES TO CRITICISM. WE FEED OFF OF IT."

James

In July 1984 *Ride The Lightning* was released on Megaforce (in America) and Music For Nations (in Europe) and immediately sold better than *Kill 'Em All*, reaching No. 100 on the US album charts. With its more polished sound and diverse range of material, the album garnered yet more great reviews, forcing those who had initially written off Metallica and thrash as a mere gimmick, to reassess the band.

Cliff Burnstein and Peter Mensch of Q Prime management, who handled AC/DC and Def Leppard, were among those whose interest was piqued. Through a mutual friend, *Kerrang!* writer Xavier Russell, they contacted the band, Ulrich calling Mensch from a public phone box. The outcome was goodbye Jon Zazula, hello Q Prime. After Burnstein and Elektra Records A&R executive Michael Alago saw the band in concert, they duly signed an American deal with Elektra, who re-released *Ride The Lightning* in December. The accompanying Ride The Lightning Tour saw the band tour Europe in November and December 1984 with Tank supporting them. In January 1985 a three-month tour of the US started, with the likes of WASP and Armored

Saint. In August the band made its first appearance at the prestigious Monsters of Rock festival in the UK and appeared at the Day On The Green festival in Oakland, California.

Metallica's third album, *Master of Puppets*, was recorded at Sweet Silence studios in Copenhagen, between September and December 1985, again with Rasmussen. When released in March 1986, it shot to No. 29 in the US charts, where it would spend 72 weeks. The band supported Ozzy Osbourne in America from March to August with some headline dates in May and June. They began the European leg of their Damage Inc. Tour in the UK on September 10. Only 17 days later, in Sweden, the band's tour bus crashed leaving Ulrich, Hetfield and Hammett relatively unscathed, but Cliff Burton was thrown out and killed instantly. He was 24. With the blessing of Burton's family, they auditioned for a new bassist, and out of 40-plus auditions, they picked Flotsam and Jetsam bassist Jason Newsted, and completed the Master of Puppets Tour.

Newsted's first recording experience with the band was the *Garage*

Days Re-Revisited EP of covers, before Metallica set out on a few Monsters of Rock shows in Europe in August, supporting Deep Purple, a dream come true for Lars Ulrich.

In August 1988 the band released their fourth album, *...And Justice For All*, again with Rasmussen, now recording in Los Angeles. In between the recording and its release they set out on a US Monsters of Rock tour in the company of Van Halen, Scorpions and Kingdom Come. On days off Ulrich and Hetfield flew back to Los Angeles to co-produce it. The album hit the US Top 10 at No. 6 and No. 4 in the UK. Metallica recorded their very first promo video for the epic 'One', their first exposure on MTV. And although the band would lose out on a Grammy nomination to prog rockers Jethro Tull (of all people), the ensuing Damaged Justice tour with support from the likes of Queensrÿche and The Cult proved how far reaching their appeal was becoming. The tour kept the band on the road until September 1989 and saw them play to fans around the world, including continents and countries the band had never been to before like South America and Australia.

KILL 'EM ALL

Arguments over what was the first thrash metal album ever will rage on till time immemorial. Some people stake the claim that Queen's 1974 track 'Stone Cold Crazy' (from *Sheer Heart Attack*) was one of the first thrash songs ever – an argument that would hardly have found favour with the notoriously narrow-minded thrash metal fraternity had Metallica themselves not covered the song for *Rubáiyát* – a special album celebrating the 40th anniversary of Elektra Records, the band's American label.

Similarly argument rages within the fastidious thrash community as to who released the very first thrash demo (popular opinion points to Metal Church's 1981 *Red Skies* demo). At the end of the day it's all a bit subjective. But when it comes to the very first recognized thrash album, then Metallica's groundbreaking 1983 debut is pretty much the widely agreed benchmark.

There's little denying that the ten tracks that make up the bristlingly angry *Kill 'Em All* were the first time that many people were confronted with thrash's snarling animosity, offering up a short, sharp shock in music therapy.

The original Metallica lineup of Lars Ulrich (drums), James Hetfield (vocals/guitar), Ron McGovney (bass) and Dave Mustaine (guitar) was always a slightly loose cannon. McGovney was ousted in favour of Trauma bassist Cliff Burton in December 1982. The even looser cannon of Mustaine was replaced by Exodus guitarist Kirk Hammett, a known quantity as the two bands had played together many times back in the Bay Area.

The band's stay on the East Coast was initiated by Jon Zazula, an East Brunswick, New Jersey local and owner of an independent record store called Rock 'n' Roll Heaven. His interest in Metallica was raised when a customer brought in a copy of the *No Life 'Til Leather* demo and played it to him. Zazula, or Jonny Z. as he was also known, contacted the band and convinced them to come over to the East Coast to play some gigs and try to earn a record contract from one of the New York based record companies. As there were no takers Zazula founded his own record company called Megaforce and released the album as his label's debut release.

Having secured the deal with the brand new label, this was the Metallica line-up that entered America Music Studios in Rochester, New York on May 10, 1983 to begin work on the band's debut album with producer Paul Curcio. As one might expect, some of the material the band recorded was culled from previous bands. 'Hit The Lights,' the

RIGHT Page size advertisement for Metallica's cancelled Hell On Earth tour of the UK with The Rods and Exciter.

song that Metallica had previously recorded for the *Metal Massacre* compilation and also appeared on the *Power Metal* and *No Life 'Til Leather* demos, had been written by Hetfield's previous band Leather Charm. Dave Mustaine, who had co-writing credits on four of the album's songs, had brought a song called 'The Mechanix' with him from his band Panic. With Mustaine no longer in the band Hetfield and Ulrich re-wrote the song, changing Mustaine's original sexually tinted lyrics to that of apocalyptic doom, added a middle section and re-titled it 'The Four Horsemen'. Mustaine eventually recorded his own version, simply

entitled 'Mechanix', for Megadeth's 1985 debut album *Killing Is My Business... And Business Is Good*. ('Jump In The Fire', 'Phantom Lord' and 'Metal Militia' were the other songs on which Mustaine was credited).

While Kirk Hammett did not get any writing credits, bassist Cliff Burton had one to his name, the bass solo '(Anesthesia) Pulling Teeth'. This was the bass solo that Burton had performed with Trauma the night both Ulrich and Hetfield had seen the band at the Whisky a Go Go. Impressed with Burton's heavy distortion, lead style of playing, tapping and heavy use of wah-wah pedal, they'd asked him to join the band and

LEFT James Hetfield sporting the band's "Metal Up Your Ass" t-shirt at The Stone, March 19, 1983.

RIGHT James flipping the bird at the crowd, live in 1984.

BELOW Kirk Hammett's first SF show with Metallica at The Stone, September 3, 1983.

the song would become Burton's trademark live solo spot in Metallica.

The breakneck speed and articulate precision of the likes of 'Hit The Lights', 'Jump In The Fire' and the defiantly pro-metal anthem 'Whiplash' went a long way to securing Metallica's place as leading lights with the burgeoning thrash metal crowd, *Kill 'Em All* contained at least two bona fide classics that have gone on to transcend the thrash tag and stand as genuine metal anthems. 'The Four Horseman''s inherent melody, something which still shines through despite the ferocity of the material (one major factor which always set Metallica apart from their thrash peers) simply reeks of class. While on 'Seek And Destroy', the

band's passion for Diamond Head, more so than any other NWOBHM band, is clear for all to hear.

Metallica originally wanted to call the album "Metal Up Your Ass", and intended on featuring a toilet bowl with a hand clutching a shining knife blade reaching out from it on the album's sleeve. Needless to say, this met with resistance from distributors, and Megaforce urged the band to rethink. They settled on *Kill 'Em All* in reference to an offhand comment from Cliff Burton with regard to the aforementioned distributors. The band did, however, produce a t-shirt with the original "Metal Up Your Ass" design on it.

Kill 'Em All was released on July 25, 1983 on Megaforce in the US and Music For Nations in the UK. Although largely ignored by the mainstream, underground magazines such as Holland's *Aardschok* (the first outside of the US to write about the band), UK's *Metal Forces*, (which promoted the thrash metal cause over the next few years in the UK) and Germany's *Rock Hard* were quick to champion the band. Even though Southern Californian compatriots Slayer would release their debut *Show No Mercy* on Brian Slagel's Metal Blade label in December, throwing down something of a gauntlet to Metallica, in truth, with *Kill 'Em All*, Metallica had already raced well ahead of any chasing pack.

CLIFF BURTON

What would have happened to Metallica had Cliff Burton not died so tragically that night of September 26, 1986? It's a question many Metallica fans have often pondered.

Born Clifford Lee Burton on February 10, 1962, in Castro Valley, California, Burton's early years were a mix of calm and tragedy too. A passionate love of music began when his own father introduced him to classical music and Burton began piano lessons. His love of classical music never left him, and was said to be the inspiration behind Metallica's decision to work with an orchestra for the *S&M* live album. Burton's musical taste developed, encompassing rock music, especially blues, country and southern rock and eventually heavy metal, as well as a liking for jazz. It was this open-minded and free-thinking approach that clearly gave Burton the edge over his thrash metal contemporaries.

However his early years were also tainted by tragedy when, aged 13, Burton's elder brother Scott tragically died at the age of 16. This incident propelled the young Burton toward the bass guitar, which he took to with gusto, his parents recalling how he claimed, in the wake of Scott's passing, "I'm going to be the best bassist for my brother" and he took to practising for up to six hours a day.

RIGHT Bang That Head That Doesn't Bang. An early live shot of Cliff, 1983.

BELOW Cliff playing live during the Damage Inc. tour at Pine Knob Amphitheatre, Michigan, July 21, 1986.

ABOVE A classic shot of Cliff, establishing his relaxed hippy image.

RIGHT Cliff Burton enjoying himself onstage at Donington 1985.

One of Burton's earliest bands was with schoolmates and eventual Faith No More members Jim Martin and Mike Bordin, EZ-Street, named after a local topless bar. Burton's own ambitions swiftly outgrew that of his bandmates. There is rehearsal footage from this time which gives fascinating insight into the development of Burton's playing style, which was more about using the bass as an individual instrument rather than merely part of the rhythm section. His next outing, however, would have far more impact in the world of heavy metal.

Trauma was Burton's first major band. They were signed to guitar-shred maestro Mike Varney's Shrapnel Records, and took the more standard heavy metal of Iron Maiden and played it at a much higher tempo. In reality they were a kind of proto thrash band, but even within that framework, Burton's foresight stood out. Trauma followed Metallica, appearing on the second *Metal Massacre* compilation album with the song 'Such A Shame'. Within Trauma, Burton further developed his solo, and it was this, "stunning shredding" according to James Hetfield, that really caught the ear of both himself and Lars Ulrich when they caught Trauma playing live at the legendary Whisky a Go Go club on Sunset Boulevard. With the pair questioning the role of original bassist Ron McGovney, watching this flare-wearing, denim-clad character conjure such

astounding sounds from his instrument had an immediate impact. They decided they wanted Cliff Burton in their band.

"We heard this wild solo going and thought 'I don't see a guitar player up there,'" James recalled to *Rolling Stone* in 1993. "It turned out it was the bass player, with a wah-wah pedal and this mop of hair." Burton turned down the band's initial overtures, but with Lars Ulrich's persistence and tenacity, he eventually succumbed, although he did demand that they relocate to San Francisco. Most bands would probably have baulked at the suggestion. It is a measure of Hetfield and Ulrich's awe of Burton that they readily agreed. In hindsight, had Metallica never seen Cliff Burton on stage, nor moved to the thriving Bay Area, this story may have panned out a much different way.

Likewise the night of September 26, 1986. Metallica were in high spirits after playing a blinder of a show on their Damage Inc. world tour

in Stockholm, Sweden. That night in the early hours of the morning of September 27 the bus skidded, Cliff Burton was thrown through the window of the bus, which then toppled over, landing on top off him. Aged 24, Cliff Burton was dead.

In death his legacy has grown – Dave Mustaine wrote 'In My Darkest Hour' in Burton's memory. But it is his inspiration to Metallica where Cliff Burton's legacy truly lives. Hetfield and Ulrich may have been the leaders of the band, but they too looked up to their bass player and recognized that his musical prowess and insight would be that which could help take Metallica above and beyond those that ultimately followed. Never again would Metallica sound quite as thrilling, as progressive and as exciting as they did on the three albums they recorded with Cliff Burton in the band.

Metallica went on to become the biggest heavy metal band on the planet. But without Cliff Burton, they would never be quite the same.

RIDE THE LIGHTNING

"We don't want to repeat what's gone before. We've done *Kill 'Em All*. If that's what people want, they've got it. No, we're ready to move on. I think this will appeal to a wider audience."

These were the words Lars Ulrich uttered when considering Metallica's second album, *Ride The Lightning* at the time. And they give us a very good view of the mindset of the band, a view that looked way beyond the confines of the thrash metal genre that Metallica were, in the wake of their debut album *Kill 'Em All*, seen as figureheads of, and at a much broader picture – one that would reach a creative apotheosis with 1990s Metallica, and seemingly be the guiding principle for the band at least until the turn of the century and dawn of a new millennium.

For there is little doubt about the enormous leap that Metallica made with *Ride The Lightning*. Whilst most Metallica fans would point to *Master of Puppets*, or perhaps even to *Metallica*, as being the defining musical moment of Metallica's career, *Ride The Lightning* is even more astounding when one considers that the band were a mere three years old, their studio time had been limited (*Kill 'Em All* had been recorded during a period of just over two weeks in Rochester, New York), and despite the fact they were racking up an impressive amount of time on the road – they'd already supported the likes of Y&T, Raven, Saxon and Venom, as well as their own increasingly impressive live shows – most apocryphal tales from the world of rock suggest that a band's second album is always the 'awkward' one. Not so Metallica...

The band had been earnestly working on new material as early as September 1983, a mere two months after the release of *Kill 'Em All*, and when it came to enter a recording studio, the band looked a bit further afield than New York. The success of *Kill 'Em All*, plus the fact that the band were now signed in Europe to the Music For Nations label meant that budgets were slightly larger, and Metallica found themselves in Copenhagen's Sweet Silence Studios with studio owner Flemming Rasmussen, who would be the album's engineer and co-producer on *Ride The Lightning*.

It wasn't all plain sailing of course. The added pressure of recording in another country (although at least Lars would have felt at home) might have taken its toll on the rest of the band (although

any potential language barrier would have allowed Lars to strengthen his position alongside Hetfield at the helm of the young metalheads). What certainly did upset things was having a lot of their equipment stolen in January 1984, following a show in Boston that got cancelled due to extremely bad weather. As a blessing in disguise the band had taken most of their instruments into the hotel as they were afraid the extreme cold would damage them, but a lot of other equipment was lost when their van got stolen from the hotel's parking lot that night. Hetfield in particular was hit hard by the theft, losing a prized Marshall guitar amplifier through which he had worked hard to develop his sound. In the end, the fact that the band were recording in Denmark paid dividends when the guitarist found a replacement in a Danish music store.

When it came to recording, the process ran relatively smoothly, the band warming to their new surroundings and working with a new co-producer (Ulrich being particularly impressed that Rasmussen had worked with UK heavy rockers Rainbow). When it was released in July 1984, *Ride The Lightning* had immediate impact. It doesn't matter when one listens to this quite splendid album within the timeframe of Metallica's history – the advancement the band had made within one year of their debut is electrifying, not simply in musical terms but in their overall approach to creating music. Whether this was down to the increased involvement of guitarist Kirk Hammett, who on the epic 'Fade To Black' garnered his first ever writing credit for the band, is a matter of conjecture. The song itself was, in part, inspired by the band's equipment theft, with James Hetfield noting that "I wrote that song at a friend's house in New Jersey. I was pretty depressed at the time because our gear had just been stolen, and we had been thrown out of our manager's house for breaking shit and drinking his liquor cabinet dry. It's a suicide song, and we got a lot of flak for it, as if kids were killing themselves because of the song. But we also got hundreds of letters from kids telling us how they related to the song and that it made them feel better."

ABOVE Some serious posing in front of a backdrop with the *Ride The Lightning* artwork.

OPPOSITE ABOVE Flyer for the first ever UK show – March 27, 1984.

'Fade To Black', a long-time staple part of Metallica's live set since, was just one of several real gems on *Ride The Lightning* that displayed the immense push onwards the band had made since *Kill 'Em All*. The driving 'Creeping Death', with its lyrical themes of Biblical plague, remains one of the band's finest ever songs and was the tour single for the European part of the Ride The Lightning Tour. It got Hammett his second writing credit on the album as the middle section of the song was taken directly from a song called 'Die By His Hand' that Hammett had written while he was still in his previous band Exodus. The classic 'For Whom The Bell Tolls' that starts with a haunting bell tolling was inspired by Ernest Hemingway's 1940 novel of the same name. The band considered releasing it as a single and even recording a video for it but in the end the plan was disbanded and only a promotional 12" for radio playback saw the light of day.

These three songs in particular stand out, but they were backed up with material that was still head and shoulders above that which the band's contemporaries were coming up with. Openers 'Fight Fire With Fire' and the title track showed that whilst the band's over-all sound was more accomplished, they could still thrash away, whilst the claustrophobic 'Trapped Under Ice' echoes the nightmarish visions of its lyrical content and closing instrumental, 'The Call Of Ktulu' (Dave Mustaine's only credit on the album along with the title track), highlighted an interest in the works of horror author H. P. Lovecraft.

It was on the melodic, almost balladic 'Escape' that the band really showed how far they were prepared to go to progress. Whilst some of the material on *Ride The Lightning* hinted at slower tempos and a more progressive approach to songwriting, here the band really broke the mould for a perceived thrash band, forcing some of the more narrow-minded amongst their audience to accuse the band of selling out. In hindsight, Hetfield was not too happy with the result either, refusing to play it live right up until the band's own Orion festival in 2012 where they finally played the complete album in its entirety.

"This time we've learnt that it is possible to slow down the pace without losing any power," said Ulrich at the time. "We have got intensity still, but there's also subtlety. It's moving in a new direction."

Indeed it was, onwards and upwards. The album reached No. 100 in the US *Billboard* chart and 87 in the UK album charts. It has since sold over five million copies. Metallica had arrived, leaving thrash metal trailing in their immense wake.

RIGHT Fully signed flyer for the 1983/1984 New Year's Eve show in Mt. Vernon, New York, USA.

OVERLEAF Individual band member shots in front of the same *Ride The Lightning* backdrop.

ONLY UK APPEARANCE

METALLICA

marquee

90 WARDOUR STREET W.1.

TUESDAY 27TH MARCH

DOOR 7.30 P.M. **TICKETS £3.00.**

THIS NEW YEAR'S EVE THE LEFT BANK STARTS OFF 1984...
WITH A DOUBLE BARRELED BLAST OF HOT HEAVY METAL

METALLICA
AND SPECIAL GUEST
ANTHRAX
DOORS OPEN 10 P.M. SAT. DEC. 31

$10 ADMISSION INCLUDES FREE CHAMPAGNE AT MIDNITE
PARTY FAVORS FREE MUNCHIES, AND LOTS OF FUN

THE LEFT BANK LISTEN TO WLIR FOR OUR ADS
THE LEFT BANK 20 E. 1ST ST. MT. VERNON N.Y. (914)90-6618

HELL-BENT GRAFIX
DESIGN: M.W. SEDDON

KIRK HAMMETT

He may be one of the quiet ones in Metallica, but being within the ranks of one of the most famous heavy metal bands ever is not something Kirk Hammett takes lightly. Indeed, it was a dream for him to join the band from the very minute he first laid eyes on them.

"I saw them at the Old Waldorf in San Francisco and they were opening up for Laaz Rockit," he recalled to *Kerrang!* "They came on and just blew the place apart. Everyone who saw them that night was converted. By the time Laaz Rockit came to play, three-quarters of the crowd had left.

"Within the first few minutes of seeing them I thought to myself, 'These guys are so goddamn original, but that guitar player isn't so hot, they should get me'. That was really strange, because two or three months later I got that phone call to join."

Kirk Lee Hammett was born in San Francisco on November 18, 1962, to a Philippino mother and an Irish merchant seaman father. Music, specifically the burgeoning heavy metal scene, would prove to be a safe haven and outlet for a childhood which was far from easy.

RIGHT At the Poperinge Festival, Belgium in 1984.

LEFT Kirk enjoying a cold beer backstage while on tour in 1984.

OPPOSITE Kirk and Lars with Jason, backstage on tour in 1987.

"WE'RE DOING IT OUR WAY. WE HAVEN'T HAD TO CONFORM TO ANY CERTAIN STANDARDS. WE DID IT ALL OURSELVES." *Kirk*

"James comes from a broken home, and I come from a broken home," Kirk told *Playboy* magazine in 2001. "When I joined the band we kind of bonded over that. I was abused as a child. My dad drank quite a lot. He beat the shit out of me and my mom quite a bit. I got hold of a guitar and from the time I was 15 I rarely left my room. I remember having to pull my dad off my mom when he attacked her during my 16th birthday – he turned on me and started slapping me around. Then my dad just left one day. My mom was struggling to support me and my sister. I've definitely channelled a lot of anger into music."

Amid such dysfunctionality, it is no surprise that the young Hammett immersed himself in music and the guitar. He attended De Anza High School in Richmond, California, where he was close friends with Les Claypool, later of Primus. Hammett's first guitar was a Fender Stratocaster copy purchased from a Montgomery Ward catalogue but it wasn't long until he'd progressed to a 1974 Gibson Flying V, and, once he'd saved enough money to purchase the obligatory Marshall amp, he decided to quit his job at Burger King.

For a young metal-inspired guitarist (tutored by Joe Satriani no less) in San Francisco in the early 1980s, the options weren't exactly extensive. But there was an underground movement afoot, inspired by the heavy metal sound emanating across the Atlantic from the UK. A new force in metal was rising in San Francisco, fired on by the likes of Judas Priest and Motörhead and the newer sounds of bands like Iron Maiden and Diamond Head. Turning their backs on the once hip but now bloated 1970s rock acts such as (at the time) Aerosmith and Montrose, the youth of the Bay Area were restless and looking for something new and exciting. Adapting these influences into their own style, they found it in thrash metal.

Hammett started out in a band called Mesh but by 1980 he'd formed Exodus with fellow guitarist Tim Agnello, bassist Carlton Meson, drummer Tom Hunting and vocalist Keith Stewart. By 1981 Hammett's guitar tech Gary Holt was a member as was vocalist Paul Baloff, and it was this trio, along with drummer Hunting and bassist Jeff Andrews (who would soon leave to form Possessed) that recorded the 1982 *Demo*, the only Exodus recording to ever feature Hammett on guitar.

By February 1983 Metallica had moved into a house in the Bay Area owned by Mark Whittaker, who also managed Exodus. Already Dave Mustaine's drinking and mood swings were causing problems for Metallica. By the time they'd spent the $1,500 the Zazulas had sent them to get to New York to record their debut album, his place within their ranks was seriously under question. The band had first played with Exodus when they'd opened for Metallica in November 1982. Exodus also supported Metallica at Cliff's first ever show with the band. Some rumours allege Kirk was invited to join Metallica then. Whatever, by the time Dave Mustaine was put on a coach back to San Francisco, Kirk Hammett was flying out to take his place on debut *Kill 'Em All*.

Hammett has truly blossomed since joining Metallica. His incendiary soloing is integral to the band's sound, and it's worth remembering that 'Creeping Death', one of Metallica's finest ever songs, began life as the Hammett-penned Exodus song 'Die By The Sword'.

Outside of Metallica, Hammett has worked with his pal Les Claypool, Santana and even UK dance act Orbital, as well as voicing his own character in *The Simpsons* and performing as other characters on the Cartoon Network show *Adult Swim*. Hammett studied Film and Asian Arts at San Francisco State University in Metallica's downtime between *Metallica* and *Load*. And, as a horror film fan, he's released a book entitled *Too Much Horror Business: The Kirk Hammett Collection*, documenting his huge collection of horror memorabilia. A man of many talents, but it's Hammett tearing up his ESP that Metallica fans really want to see, against a wall of classic sounding heavy metal.

MASTER OF PUPPETS

Is *Master of Puppets* the best Metallica album ever? Is it the greatest heavy metal album ever? Although these might be subjective questions, let's face it, *Master of Puppets* does stand against some stiff competition, not least from the band's own 1991 album *Metallica*.

There's little denying the power and impact that the album made when it came out. With little or no promotion whatsoever, a move instigated by the band who had never even made a promotional video at this point, Metallica's bullish stance paid off, with *Master of Puppets* crashing into the US charts at No. 29 (and a more than respectable 41 in the UK).

Recorded once again at Copenhagen's Sweet Silence Studios with Flemming Rasmussen, with whom the band had worked so effectively on *Ride The Lightning*, this time Metallica allowed themselves far more time to work on their new record – almost four months as opposed to just over a fortnight. They had begun writing material for their third album almost as soon as they'd come off the road in support of *Ride The Lightning* in March 1985. In the interim period between then and entering Sweet Silence in September the band made their very first appearance at Donington's Monsters of Rock festival, headlined by ZZ Top. Metallica's position lower on the bill in between bands like Ratt,

ABOVE LEFT Burton, Ulrich, Hetfield and Hammett posing in front of the stage set-up for the Damage Inc. tour.

LEFT Silver Phonogram hipflask. Monsters of Rock, Donington, 1987.

ABOVE Hammett and Hetfield at the Monsters of Rock festival in Pforzheim, Germany, August 30, 1987.

Magnum and Bon Jovi provoked Hetfield's now infamous on stage rant declaring what kind of band the crowd was looking at: "If you came here to see spandex and fucking eye make-up and all that shit and the words 'rock 'n' roll baby' in every song, this ain't the fucking band!" The band's stall was further increased when they also appeared at the prestigious Day on the Green festival in Oakland, California on Saturday August 31 alongside Scorpions, Ratt and Y&T. Although the recording of *Master of Puppets* must have seemed interminably lengthy to a

band who until that point had never spent beyond a couple of weeks recording anything, it's worth noting that Metallica were something of a well-oiled machine when setting about recording their third album. But the experience of their previous two albums, not to mention the significant creative advancement they'd shown between both releases, served Metallica well.

It needed to as well. For although sometimes there seems to be an element of criticism aimed at *Master of Puppets* that it didn't really show enough development in terms of sequencing and lyrical themes as its predecessor, the very fact that the far more complex arrangements and introduction of layering in vocal harmonies and more melodic guitar sequences demanded by the band's new material display just why more time was required to work on the new songs – *Master of Puppets* shows another significant step on from the progression the band had already made.

Everything about *Master of Puppets* attains to the epic. It is the sound of a band who, having smashed down the boundaries of thrash they felt so constrained by on *Ride The Lightning*, now feel they operate with few or no boundaries at all. Thankfully, the band's youth and ardent metal fandom, and support of abrasive metal sounds, meant we didn't end up with some sprawling prog metal epic, but probably the most direct and forceful heavy metal statement since Motörhead unleashed *Ace of Spades* some five years previous.

Opening with a flourish of Spanish acoustic guitar 'Battery' soon smashes its way through the speakers to begin the delivery of eight more incisively excellent slices of heavy metal. Up there with the precision of the opening cut are the eight minutes plus of sheer brilliance of the album's title track with its layered signature guitar part in the middle. The epic build up of 'Welcome Home (Sanitarium)', penned by Hetfield in tribute to the film *One Flew Over The Cuckoo's Nest* is one of the other stand out tracks. These three tracks, much like 'Creeping Death', 'Fade To Black' and 'For Whom The Bell Tolls' on *Ride The Lightning*, would go on to be remembered as definitive Metallica classics.

ABOVE Hetfield (left) and Hammett live during the Damage Inc. tour in support of *Master of Puppets*.

RIGHT Backstage baloney on tour at the Iowa Jam in Des Moines, Iowa, May 1986.

And yet just like the album's predecessor, the remaining five tracks are no slouches either. 'The Thing That Should Not Be' was another nod to the band's love of author H.P. Lovecraft, whilst the brutally heavy 'Disposable Heroes', a track the band had premiered live at a German festival back in September 1985, again played on lyrical themes concerned with the futility of war. With 'Leper Messiah''s attack on TV evangelism, it showed that some of the more phantasmagorical lyrical ideas of *Kill 'Em All* had been left far behind. *Master of Puppets* also featured the stunning instrumental 'Orion', a piece that was largely orchestrated by Cliff Burton and displayed an innate sense of developing musicianship from the band.

Ironically, the album's closing track, 'Damage Inc.', was about as thrash metal as Metallica ever got, and yet everything else on *Master of Puppets* pointed Metallica ever further away from a genre they considered too claustrophobic and no longer a part of. "From a musician's point of view I don't like the term," Lars Ulrich told *Kerrang!* magazine. "It implies lack of arrangement, lack of ability, lack of songwriting." With a highly acclaimed new album under their belt the band set out on their first real world tour that was supposed to take them to unexplored territory, but little did they know what awaited them within a mere nine months.

BELOW Fun and games during the band's first time in Japan, Nov. 1986.

RIGHT The band as tourists in front of Osaka Castle, Osaka, Japan. November 18, 1986.

...AND JUSTICE FOR ALL

"Perfect," said *Rolling Stone* magazine. "Except for its lack of memorable songs."
Even without the benefit of hindsight, one would have to conclude that judgement a little on the harsh side. True, *...And Justice For All* might be one of Metallica's least accessible albums (outside of *St. Anger*), but when one considers the circumstances surrounding its recording then that might go some way to explaining why some people perceive the album as being one of the band's weakest sounding albums, or creatively overblown.

There's certainly no denying that, sandwiched in between the electrifying run of Metallica's first three albums and the bottom-end heavy yet polished production of *Metallica*, *...And Justice For All* sounds pretty reed thin soundwise. And yet, despite what *Rolling Stone* had to say, it also contains some of Metallica's finest songs and certainly the most progressive (in terms of song structure, rather than keyboard solos and week long songs) writing the band had come up with to date.

However, by the time the band entered the One On One Studio in Los Angeles on January 28, 1988, they were a band in a state of flux. The success of 1986's *Master of Puppets* album had catapulted the band into the big league, snapping at the heels of arena status. And yet it was a mere 16 months since the tragic death of bassist Cliff Burton. As has happened with so many bands before them, as great success came calling, that fickle mistress Fate handed out a terrible reminder of the flip side of the coin.

Although Metallica have always revolved via the axis of James Hetfield and Lars Ulrich (being the two constants who formed Metallica), Cliff Burton was an integral part of the musicality of the band. It was he who consistently impressed his fellow band mates with his instrumental prowess. It was his own bass solo '(Anesthesia) Pulling Teeth' that so wowed Hetfield and Ulrich at an LA Trauma gig that they pursued him to join their band. And it was his arrangement that made 'Orion' on *Master of Puppets* stand out so much.

It was 'Orion' too that was played at Burton's funeral in Castro Valley on October 7, 1986, after which his family gave Metallica their blessing to carry on. Just over a month after Burton had so tragically died, Metallica announced that ex-Flotsam And Jetsam bassist, 23-year old Jason Newsted, was his replacement. For Newsted, joining these ever-growing metal titans was a baptism of fire. His first gig in Reseda, California less than a month after he joined, an ensuing Japanese tour and a full month of US and Canadian dates, rounded off a tumultuous year for all concerned in the band. Early 1987 saw Newsted and his new bandmates having to end the European tour that Cliff Burton had

begun. In July 1987 the whole band entered the studio to record their *Garage Days Re-Revisited* EP (dubbed the $5.98 EP after the price at which it sold) of cover versions to ease the new line-up into studio work. The day after it was released Metallica played Donington's Monsters of Rock for a second time, although their performance was nowhere near

as impressive as their first two years before. The year ended with the release of the *Cliff 'Em All* video as tribute to their departed bass player.

One can imagine it was a Metallica with mixed emotions that entered One On One with Mike Clink towards the end of January in 1988.

L'AMOUR

1546 62nd Street (between 15th & 16th Ave.) • Bayridge, N.Y. • (718) 232-1616

THE ROCK CAPITOL OF BROOKLYN

The Metal Massacre

FRIDAY, SATURDAY & SUNDAY*
JANUARY 25th, 26th & 27th*

METALLICA

WASP

Special
Guest

ARMORED SAINT

*Sunday Open to All Ages

TICKET OUTLETS

- **L'AMOUR'S BOX OFFICE**
- **MUSIC FACTORY**
  Staten Island Mall
- **ONLY ROCK 'N ROLL**
  49 W. 8th Street
  Manhattan
- **ROCK 'N ROLL HEAVEN**
  Clark, N.J.
- **ZIG ZAG RECORDS**
  Avenue U
  Brooklyn
- **TICKETRON OUTLETS**

EMA & E.T. Concerts ApS proudly present

METALLICA

special guests ANTHRAX

SOLNAHALLEN

Fredag 26 September 1986 kl. 19.30

Publikinsläpp kl. 18.30

Burkar, flaskor, kameror, bandspelare förbjudet att medföra.
Fotografering och bandupptagning förbjudet.

Pris: 110:- + förköp   Nr 0947

AUGUST 31, 1985
ALL DAY FESTIVAL

SCORPIONS
RATT
Y & T
METALLICA
RISING FORCE
FEATURING YNGWIE MALMSTEEN
VICTORY

SAT · AUG 31 2:00 P.M.

OAKLAND STADIUM

Recording ran to just over four months, only one longer than *Master of Puppets*, but ran into trouble almost immediately. Clink had been chosen owing to his work on Guns N' Roses' *Appetite For Destruction* album (released the previous year). However things did not work out and the band turned back to Flemming Rasmussen, the Danish producer who had worked on their previous two albums. In the end, Clink ended up being credited for engineering the drum sound and helping in the recording of two covers, Budgie's 'Breadfan' and Diamond Head's 'The Prince', which would appear as B-sides.

When *...And Justice For All* did appear, on August 25, 1988, there's no denying the instant success the fourth Metallica album garnered, immediately shoving its creators into the arena league. The album crashed into the *Billboard* album chart at No. 6. In the UK it went two

better, reaching No. 4. And yet it also left fans scratching their heads. There was no denying the quality of material like 'Harvester Of Sorrow', 'Blackened' or 'The Shortest Straw'. And yet where Ulrich's drums had previously sounded rock solid, here they sounded taut and thin. The guitars razored away, but Newsted's bass was rendered almost negligible. And can one read into the themes of raging social injustice and a decaying American civilisation to be found from the album cover and title to the bitter lyrical content, a Metallica exorcising demons left from Burton's own tragic death?

At times, *...And Justice For All* almost sounds like a thrash band trying to sound like prog rock act King Crimson (Hammett was a massive fan), such were the complex time changes to be found on the record. And yet it was the ominously building, balladic 'One', based on Dalton Trumbo's novel *Johnny Got His Gun* that the band found their greatest yet success.

It was for this song the band filmed their first ever promo video at an abandoned LA warehouse on December 6, 1988 (besides purchasing the rights of the 1971 film of the novel so they could use footage in the harrowing video). A distilled version was sent to MTV, 'One' was a huge hit single for the band (No. 13 in the UK Top 40 no less).

'To Live Is To Die', the album's haunting lengthy instrumental was a final nod to Burton. The title was from a phrase Burton would often use, the eerie vocal lines taken not from his own poetry, as has been written, but in fact the biggest part of the lyrics came from a Paul Gerhardt poem used in the 1981 fantasy film *Excalibur*. It was the only Metallica instrumental ever to feature his replacement Newsted.

The album's closing track 'Dyer's Eve' would prove to be the band's last convulsion of anything even remotely close to thrash metal for the next two decades.

THE 1990s

Given the hectic pace of the 1980s, coloured for Metallica with both triumph and tragedy, by comparison the 1990s was a far different kind of decade altogether. On one hand, they found themselves at the very top of their game, sat astride the whole metal world...

FAR LEFT Metallica live at Woodstock, August 13, 1994.

LEFT Jason Newsted throwing the horns.

On the other, their studio work rate slowed down (no surprise there, as this is a common occurrence with many bands as their careers take off), releasing just three new studio albums, alongside a massive live box set plus a compilation of covers and a symphonic live album, whilst they also spend much of the decade on the road. To others, the 1990s was the decade when Metallica finally, ultimately sold out and lost their mojo (accusations that would be levelled at the band throughout the following decade).

The 1980s ended in a way which perhaps summed up how the preceding decade had gone for the band. They began 1989 losing out to prog rockers Jethro Tull for a Grammy Award for Best Hard Rock/ Heavy Metal performance, but ended with the news that not only had *...And Justice For All* just passed the two million sales mark, but their *2 Of One* video (a VHS that ran for under 20 minutes and featured two versions of the 'One' promo video and an introduction by Lars) had also passed the platinum mark for sales.

The new decade began in fairly low-key fashion for the band however. They'd recorded a cover of Queen's proto-thrash song 'Stone Cold Crazy' for the *Rubáiyát* album to celebrate the 40th anniversary of their US label Elektra. In May they ventured to Europe to play some festival dates, preceded by an unannounced appearance as support to Metal Church at London's Marquee Club. In August Lars and James began recording demos for the band's next album, which they began recording with producer Bob Rock in October. The band continued working on the new album for the first half of 1991, releasing the album on August 12, 1991 to enormous fanfare and immense commercial success. A week before, some 10,000 fans packed out Madison Square Garden simply to hear the new work, giving an indication of just how popular the band had become. A week after the album's release Metallica made their third appearance at Donington's Monsters of Rock, performing a slightly lacklustre yet well received performance as direct support to headliners AC/DC. In September the two bands also appeared at

a massive rock concert at Moscow's Tushino Airfield, that had an estimated crowd of close to a million people. In October they kicked off the massive, 21-month Wherever We May Roam world tour, that also included an appearance at the Freddie Mercury Tribute Concert at Wembley Stadium on April 20, 1992 (the band performed 'Enter Sandman', 'Sad But True' and 'Nothing Else Matters', James Hetfield played 'Stone Cold Crazy' with the remaining members of Queen and Black Sabbath's riffmeister Tony Iommi), and a somewhat rancorous co-headline tour with Guns N' Roses, during which James was badly burned on stage in a pyrotechnic accident in Montreal, Canada. After a break in the tour to give Hetfield time to recuperate the tour continued with John Marshall (Metal Church) playing Hetfield's guitar parts once again, just like he had done back in 1986 when James had broken his wrist.

Most of 1993 was also spent on the road in support of *Metallica* (*The Black Album*). The second half of the year saw Hetfield and Ulrich sifting through live recordings and producing the band's live box set

THEY SAID IT WOULD NEVER HAPPEN
GUNS N' ROSES
METALLICA

WITH SPECIAL GUEST
FAITH NO MORE

SUNDAY AUGUST 9 • 5:30PM
EXHIBITION STADIUM
ON SALE NOW

GET YOUR TICKETS AT ALL TICKETMASTER OUTLETS,
OR TO CHARGE CALL THE 24 HOUR TICKETMASTER LINE
870-8000

FOR FURTHER CONCERT DETAILS, CALL CPI'S 24 HOUR CONCERT HOTLINE 538-0088

◆ C P I ◆◆◆◆◆◆◆◆◆

LEFT Concert poster for a 1992 co-headlining show with Guns N' Roses in Toronto, Canada, "They Said It Would Never Happen". Well it didn't – this show was cancelled.

MONSTERS OF ROCK

IRON MAIDEN
METALLICA
HELLOWEEN
ANTHRAX
MANZANO

PERSONAL TECNICO

WEMBLEY
VENUE OF LEGENDS

METALLICA

WEDNESDAY
23rd MAY 1990

STANDING
AREA PASS

INVITATION
TICKET 〈非売品〉

UDO
ARTISTS, INC

CONCERT FINAL COUNTDOWN
12月31日 時
5:00

PLACE 東京ドーム(ビッグ・エッグ)

スタンド 階 B7 列 86

FINAL COUNTDOWN 1991
METALLICA
EUROPE TESLA
THUNDER

主催:日本テレビ/TOKYO FM

UDO ARTISTS. INC. 03-3402-7281
東京ドーム 21ゲート
1991.12.31 (火)
3:30PM 開場 5:00PM 開演
アリーナ S ¥7,000【消費税込み】
11124 58869 C16 ブロック 179番
KBE011002201 チケットぴあ さいか屋横須賀店

FAR LEFT Working Pass for a Monsters of Rock show in Spain, opening for Iron Maiden, September 1988.

BOTTOM LEFT/RIGHT Invitation tickets for the New Year's Eve show in Tokyo, Japan, December 31, 1991.

LEFT Standing Area Pass for the Wembley Arena show in London, England, May 23, 1990.

OPPOSITE LEFT James Hetfield taking a break during the recording of *Metallica*.

OPPOSITE RIGHT James sweating it off, on tour for *The Black Album*.

Live Shit:Binge & Purge that featured three full live shows, two on video and one on CD or cassette.

1994 saw the band head out on a massive US summer tour, on which the band headlined one of the days of the Woodstock festival in August. Metallica began work on their sixth studio album in May 1995, again with Bob Rock, although this time the band used Sausalito's Plant Studios. Within months they were back out on the road for a handful of dates dubbed Escape From The Studio '95, during which the band played a fan club-only show at London's Astoria and finally made their first (and overdue) headline appearance at Donington (supported by Therapy?, Skid Row, Slayer, Slash's Snakepit, White Zombie, Machine Head, Warrior Soul and Corrosion of Conformity). In December the band paid tribute to Motörhead's Lemmy Killmister by showing up at his 50th birthday bash in Los Angeles playing a set of six Motörhead classics, all dressed up as the main guest of the evening, complete with sunglasses, wigs and moustaches.

The following year proved to be somewhat of a challenge for both the band and its fans. The new album *Load* sounded even more mainstream and blues-based than *Metallica* had done and inspired another sell-out backlash that the band had seen before when they featured 'Escape' on *Ride The Lightning*. Not only that, but the band also underwent something of a dramatic makeover which included eyeliner, more stylish, mainstream outfits and even arty black and white press shots taken by Dutch photographer Anton Corbijn, best known for his work with U2 and Depeche Mode. The first glimpse of the band's new look for their fan base came with the release of the video of the single for 'Until It Sleeps', a song with as much commercial appeal as 'Enter Sandman' had. For the band's hardcore fans, the signs weren't good.

Not that any of this hindered the band's commercial success. *Load* spent four weeks at the top spot on the *Billboard* chart and the accompanying Poor Touring Me Tour saw them play sold-out shows around the world.

In July 1997 the band re-entered Sausalito's Plant Studios to rework some of the extra material from the *Load* sessions, having decided against making *Load* a double album. This they released as *ReLoad* in November 1997, which again topped the charts, but was regarded in less favourable light by fans who had already turned their backs on *Load*. Regardless, Metallica remained a massive live draw, if not the biggest metal band on the planet throughout all this time, and their Poor Re-Touring Me Tour lasted until September 1998.

They went straight into the studio to record some new cover versions to add to the many covers the band had previously recorded throughout

their career that were released as *Garage Inc.* in November 1998. Although it only made it to No. 2 on the *Billboard* chart, the album has since gone on to sell over two and a half million copies. Not bad going for a double album of cover versions. To promote the album the band played five intimate US shows playing only covers. The opening act was Battery, a cover band playing a set consisting of only Metallica tracks.

Metallica ended the decade with a move which again challenged a lot of diehard fans, when they announced in January 1999 that they planned to perform two concerts with the San Francisco Symphony Orchestra with the late Michael Kamen conducting. The shows took place in April at the Berkeley Community Theatre, and the ensuing album (and accompanying DVD), *S&M*, was released in November. Again, the album, in this case a live album, hit the second spot on the *Billboard* album charts. Around its release the band played two more

shows with an orchestra to sold-out crowds in Berlin and New York. It seemed no matter what this metal juggernaut turned their hands to turned to gold, no matter how many detractors railed against them. Unfortunately, it could not, and would not last!

OPPOSITE Preparing for battle – soundcheck at London's Astoria 2, August 23, 1995.

ABOVE Pre-show warm-up with (L to R) Hetfield, Hammett and John Marshall, summer 1992.

METALLICA (THE BLACK ALBUM)

When an album has sold over 30 million copies worldwide, debuting at number one in ten countries (including the US, where it was the band's first album to top the *Billboard* charts), what can really be said about it?

In the case of "The Black Album", the more popular title by which Metallica's self-titled fifth album has come to be universally known, a fair bit actually. It remains one of the best known metal albums ever released, is certainly Metallica's best-known musical statement, and in true Metallica style, it pissed off the purists!

1988's *...And Justice For All*, the band's first album with new bassist Jason Newsted had been a successful album for the band, but it's questionable production sound left some fans wondering where Metallica might be headed. It was evidently something Metallica were thinking too, for despite the album's success, positioning the band on the coat tails of greatness, one couldn't hear Newsted's bass (Newsted has responded that his bass lines were following rhythm guitar lines instead). But worse still was Lars Ulrich's drum sound. Never the most technically gifted sticksman in the world, nevertheless Ulrich's forcefully pounding drums were a pivotal part of Metallica's early sound, and on *...And Justice For All* they lacked real punch.

Maybe this was the reason that Flemming Rasmussen, the Danish producer who'd worked on the past three albums had been jettisoned for album number five. Maybe Metallica just wanted to move on all round. Either way the choice of producer for *Metallica* would certainly send shockwaves around the band's diehard fan base.

Bob Rock was a man who was better known for producing Motley Crue's *Dr. Feelgood* and The Cult's *Sonic Temple*, hit albums in their own right, but the very antithesis of what a band like Metallica were supposedly all about. The fact that the likes of Bon Jovi, David Lee Roth and Blue Murder also featured on his CV hardly made him Mr. Popular amongst Metallica's fans. The band just wanted him to mix the album, but Rock stipulated he'd produce it as well. In the end, however, as Lars pointed out, "We felt that we still had our best record in us and Bob Rock could help us make it."

Recording did not go smoothly. Used to working with one producer, and probably more than aware of how important the new album was to them, Metallica were resistant to Rock's working practices, which inevitably would have differed to what they had been used to with Rasmussen. Given that this was Rock's first time working with

Metallica, he was eager to make everything work. But introducing ideas previously alien to the band led to arguments (some of which can be seen on the long form VHS *A Year And A Half In The Life Of Metallica* – the band's own move to keep the connection with their fans they clearly were aware would become more strained the bigger they got). And the fact that Ulrich, Hammett and Newsted were all going through divorces while the album was being recorded hardly helped matters.

On June 16, after almost seven months of recording (and three remixes costing a reported $1m), and with both sides claiming never to work together again, the album was complete. And on August 12, the band unleashed *Metallica* on the world. Expectations were running high. And the band were repaid with the album becoming not just their most successful to date, but in time, their most successful ever.

With no less than five hit singles lifted off the album it became an absolute classic. Fired on by the perfect heavy metal song – the, eerie, ominous, slow-building yet heavy and catchy 'Enter Sandman', Metallica smashed through the walls of the mainstream. Both the album's ballads 'The Unforgiven' and 'Nothing Else Matters' were big hits on both sides of the Atlantic, which moved Metallica into balladic areas hitherto untouched. Equally robust and heavy are the thudding likes of 'Sad But True', 'Wherever I May Roam' and 'The God That Failed'.

To commemorate the 20th anniversary of the album's release and its accompanying world tour, the band decided to honour its most successful album to date by playing it in its entirety during their own Orion Music + More festival and a handful of European dates during the summer of 2012. A most deserved honour.

LEFT Ulrich and Hetfied relaxing in the studio during the recording of the album.

OPPOSITE Hetfield during the co-headlining tour with Guns N' Roses, summer 1992.

LEFT In the studio with producer Bob Rock. (L to R) Ulrich, Rock, Hetfield.

BELOW The last show of the Roam tour. Werchter, Belgium, July 4, 1993.

OPPOSITE RIGHT Metallica's sold out Belgium Festival show, 1993, supported by a few diverse acts indeed.

OPPOSITE LEFT Flyer for the Day on the Green festival in Oakland, California, October 12, 1991.

METALLICA
DAY ON THE GREEN
QUEENSRŸCHE
FAITH NO MORE
SOUNDGARDEN
SATURDAY • OCTOBER 12
OAKLAND STADIUM • 1:30PM
TICKETS AT BASS
BILL GRAHAM PRESENTS

"I NEVER THOUGHT IT WAS POSSIBLE TO HAVE A NUMBER ONE RECORD WITH THE KIND OF MUSIC WE PLAYED."

Jason, on The Black Album

HUMO
PRESENTS
TORHOUT
WERCHTER
SATURDAY JULY 3 & SUNDAY JULY 4 '93 at 10.15 a.m.

LEVELLERS
SUGAR
THE TRAGICALLY HIP
SONIC YOUTH
THE BLACK CROWES
FAITH NO MORE
NEIL YOUNG
WITH BOOKER T AND THE MG'S
LENNY KRAVITZ
METALLICA

ROBERT TRUJILLO

"When I first heard about the job I thought to myself, 'Wow, that's interesting, that'd be a lot of fun' because I've always been a Metallica fan. I felt that I could definitely be a part of this."

This is how Robert Trujillo described his feelings about auditioning for arguably the biggest metal band on the planet to *Kerrang!* To some, the position of bassist in the band may have appeared something of a poisoned chalice, given the manner in which the media interpreted Jason Newsted's tenure in Metallica. Despite being the band's longest-serving bass player, managing 14 years with them, to the outside world it appeared as if Newsted was never truly accepted into the fold, replacing as he did the much-loved Cliff Burton.

Newsted always bore, in whispers at least, the epithet "new kid". The fact that his bass was by and large inaudible on his first proper album, *...And Justice For All*, or that he bore the brunt of many practical jokes, or even that after so long in the band he clashed with Hetfield over his desire to make a go of his Echobrain side project, the end result was that on January 17, 2001, Newsted quit Metallica.

Robert Trujillo was born on October 23, 1964 in Santa Monica, California. He grew up in the Venice Beach area of Los Angeles, where

RIGHT True dedication, playing live despite a knee injury.

BELOW Robert Trujillo giving it his best.

he developed a keen love of surfing and a passion for music, devouring anything and everything from the hard rock grooves of Led Zeppelin to swinging 1970s funk and the sweeter sounds of Motown soul. It was this acceptance of various forms of music that helped Trujillo become something beyond your standard heavy metal bass player.

Having performed in a variety of local bands, he'd also been at school with Rocky George, the guitar player in local LA punk/metal crossover act Suicidal Tendencies. George introduced Trujillo to Suicidal's leader Mike Muir. The pair hit it off and in 1989 Trujillo joined Suicidal Tendencies. He remained in the band during their most successful period, appearing on albums such as *Lights... Camera... Revolution!* and *Suicidal For Life*, before leaving to join Ozzy Osbourne's band in 1996.

However, during his tenure in Suicidal, Trujillo's evident passion for funk music intrigued Muir, and the pair formed the funk metal offshoot Infectious Grooves who made a splash in the early 1990s. The band have been on hiatus since 2000's *Mas Borracho*, although this writer would suggest seeking out the band's excellent 1991 debut album, *The Plague That Makes The Booty Move... It's The Infectious Grooves.*

To date Trujillo has also worked with Alice In Chains guitarist Jerry Cantrell, Zakk Wylde's Black Label Society (the pair having worked together in Ozzy's band), Judas Priest guitarist Glenn Tipton, on Ozzy's 2001 album *Down To Earth* and 2002's *Live At Budokan*.

Trujillo first appeared on Metallica's radar when the band toured with Suicidal Tendencies as support on 1993's Nowhere Else To Roam Tour. "Back then I was probably tighter with Jason," Trujillo would later explain. "As far as the other guys go, they were really nice to me. I remember them kicking down a bonus to Suicidal after our European tour with them, they gave each of us a thousand bucks and we were stoked. In personality terms they've grown in the last couple of years."

Trujillo's 2003 audition for Metallica features in the 2004 movie *Some Kind Of Monster*. Trujillo was up against such names as Marilyn Manson's Twiggy Ramirez, COC/Down man Pepper Keenan, and Jane's Addiction man Eric Avery. In the film, Hammett notes that like the late Cliff Burton, Trujillo plays bass with his fingers rather than a pick. On February 24, 2003 Robert Utrillo was namd as Metallica's new bassist.

Although Trujillo did not join Metallica in time to play on *St. Anger,* he was on the accompanying *St. Anger Rehearsals DVD,* a move which had him comment to *Kerrang!* magazine "I'm just happy the guys let me play the songs for the DVD part of the album. They've been really solid on making me feel part of this new album as much as possible."

Many commentators noted on how much more accepting the band appeared to be to what might have been perceived, (and in the case of Newsted certainly was the case) an outsider. Trujillo was handed a $1m advance on joining the band. For his part, there is simply no denying the added dynamism with Trujillo in the ranks, in the studio it was more than evident that Metallica were returning to their best, in terms of songwriting and overall sound. It certainly seems that Metallica had learned some serious lessons when it came to replacing personnel.

And as for Trujillo's friendship with Newsted? Ironically, as he was being offered the Metallica gig, Newsted was being offered Trujillo's own role in Ozzy Osbourne's band. The pair remain good friends. Funny how things turn out...

LOAD

The moment it really started to go wrong? Well if you believe some people, then yes, perhaps it was. Then again, these are the kind of people who, much like Garth in the film *Wayne's World*, seem to fear change.

Up until 1996, even if some diehard metal fans had moaned about the more mainstream sound of Metallica, Metallica had always represented something of a constant. Dependable defenders of the heavy metal faith. Metallica were still, for all their popularity, the people's heavy metal band. That was something many old school metal fans, always resistant to change of any kind (most likely because of the way they were treated in general by society itself), were not about to let go of in any way.

On the flip side, no one from the Metallica camp ever claimed to be doyens of the thrash massive. Nor did they ever once claim to be a thrash metal band or to play thrash until they died. They'd evolved out of a new way of thinking about creating heavy metal music and by proxy found themselves embroiled in a new movement. And yet as is the case for many forward thinking bands, surely it was their desired goal to continue to evolve as a creative unit? To become the best metal band they could be? All of which of course, involved change...

Up until 1996, any change in the creative approach of Metallica hadn't exactly been earth shattering, even if it was always accompanied by stirrings of diehard disgruntlement. However, when the band convened at Lars' own basement studio, The Dungeon, in May 1995 to begin working on new material to follow-up an album now four years old, they were faced with a dilemma. How do you follow-up an album like

Metallica? Given that progression had always been the name of the game for Metallica over their past five albums, to simply replicate that which had gone before would not only have gone against their artistic grain, but hardly have been the move fans and critics were expecting. However change too much and the knives would have inevitably been out for the band. Something of a cruel dilemma.

The fractious nature of the *Metallica* recording sessions behind them, and quite possibly buoyed by that album's immense success, Metallica and Bob Rock found themselves working together again, Rock producing with Hetfield and Ulrich, although this time at Sausalito's The Plant Studios. Metallica had 27 songs demoed for the new record and work took ten months. Indeed the band ended up with so much material, their original intention was to release a double album. However feeling that some of the new music still needed some work on it, when they got offered the headlining spot on that year's Lollapalooza festival, the band decided to release *Load* as a single album, with a follow-up, *ReLoad* to follow in its wake.

'Until It Sleeps' was chosen as the lead-off single to introduce people to the new, updated Metallica sound. Not a million miles away in feel to 'Enter Sandman', it contained a catchy enough refrain but still offered a distinctly different style of music. Released on May 21 this would be the

ABOVE LEFT James and Lars at one of the Lollapalooza gigs the band played during the summer of 1996.

ABOVE CENTRE Lars caught in the act during the Poor Touring Me tour, supporting *Load*.

ABOVE Kirk Hammett playing a solo during the Poor Touring Me tour.

first time eager fans would hear new music. On May 23 the video for the song was premiered on MTV. For the masses who hadn't picked up early news stories in the metal press (remember this was still largely pre-Internet days) it was the first chance to see the new-look Metallica. The shit duly hit the fan.

The band had cut their hair and had undergone a total make-over. Dapper suits, short back and sides, suspect moustaches, eyeliner and, in Lars' case, a feather boa, presented a completely different look for Metallica. The diehards were appalled. Upon release, the artwork for *Load*, Andres Serrano's "Semen And Blood III", in which the artist combined his own semen with bovine blood between two Plexiglas sheets, would hardly have ingratiated the band to the purists. The fact they'd altered their long-standing logo and the CD booklet full of Anton Corbijn photos, containing only snippets of lyrics within its pages, only served to outrage them even more so.

So to some extent, Metallica were fighting a losing battle before anyone even really listened to the music. Not that it seemed to really hinder their success. Plenty of fans who'd come in on the back of *Metallica* flocked to buy the new record, which duly shot to the number one spot and spent four solid weeks there.

Musically, however, the shift was nowhere near as dramatic as the band's look, it took the previous album's sound as its blueprint and moved in a bluesier blend of metal and classic rock. It was just not what some of the band's earliest fans (always the noisiest – these days we might term them trolls) wanted to hear. In truth, at least half the album is great – from the punchy opening one-two of 'Ain't My Bitch' and rolling riff of '2x4', through the aforementioned single and the hugely catchy 'Hero Of The Day' and the plaintive 'Mama Said', which allowed Hetfield to live out his outlaw country fantasies and the epic 'Bleeding Me' and 'The Outlaw Torn', this is music far better than most of Metallica's contemporaries could even hope to make.

However, at 78 minutes and 59 seconds, the album is not only the band's longest ever, just conforming to the maximum amount of music one could get on to a CD without it skipping, (something they initially proudly boasted on a sticker on the sleeve) fans tend to agree that it's probably too long by a couple of songs. In understanding that you can't please all the people all the time, with *Load* Metallica clearly set about pleasing themselves, a fact affirmed by James Hetfield who had concert crowds around the world repeat "We Don't Give A Shit" after him before plunging into the opening track of the new album. From here on, it would be a bumpy ride!

RELOAD

"We play music. You either like that music or you don't. And we do."
This was James Hetfield talking about *Load* and the follow-up, *ReLoad*. And perhaps one can sense in these words a slight irritation, or even weariness, at having to answer the many questions already asked after the release of *Load* all over again.

In truth, Hetfield was mainly responding to Lars Ulrich's proclamations to the press that Metallica were now a pop band! One should remember, perhaps that at the time Ulrich was in thrall to UK indie bands such as Oasis (if memory serves, he even took to wearing sportswear, a la hip young metal acts of the day such as Korn), and with his motormouth in full flow, he only succeeded in alienating Metallica's hardcore fanbase even further than the band's previous two albums had. Little wonder Hetfield admitted at the time that he tried not to read anything in the press where Lars was involved!

So things were, perhaps, a little fractious within the Metallica camp as the band tried to get their heads round the fall-out of (mainly) their change of appearance for 1996's *Load* album. Behind the scenes, other demons were rearing ugly heads and causing all manner of internal tension. But the fact remains that by the time *ReLoad* came out in November 1997, Metallica were more than happy to be seen in the pages of lifestyle magazines such as *Loaded*.

Against this backdrop the band went back in to The Plant studios in May 1997 to start working on the material left over from the *Load* sessions. "We wrote 27 songs for *Load* and were developing them for a double album," stated Lars at the time by way of explanation of *ReLoad*. "We then got the offer to play Lollapalooza in 1996, so we put one record out now with most of the songs that are done, and then we'll come back after a year and finish the rest of them. As far as I'm concerned you can take any of these songs and interchange them on the two albums. The only fear we had was getting to it quick. We didn't want to leave it lying around for three years and worry about what it would sound like when we came back to it."

In some ways, Ulrich was right. And why shouldn't he be? Given that all the material was written during the same sessions, then the fact that it would all be sonically linked was a no-brainer. The only problem Metallica had was that, as *Kerrang!* magazine put it at the time, "...if you didn't like *Load*, you probably won't like this one either. And *ReLoad* won't inspire anyone to change sides...." This was compounded by the fact that, although there would be later, at the time there was no

concession from the band to counter long-time fans' concerns about the band's new image. The 'androgynous cigar-toting pimp' look favoured by at least Ulrich and Hammett was still shoved remorselessly into the public eye, even if Hetfield and Newsted's new styles remained, by comparison, understated. Equally, the new style logo remained on the cover, which again bore the artwork of Andres Serrano, whilst the characteristicly artful Anton Corbijn look was splattered all across the accompanying CD booklet. But then to a certain extent, Metallica were caught between a rock and a hard place with *ReLoad*. As a companion album to *Load*, it would have looked distinctly odd to drastically alter the style, regardless of any backlash from their fans. It seems Metallica either gritted their teeth and just carried on regardless, or were happy enough to enjoy the success with the attitude that the various detractors could be damned.

The other issue was trying to prevent fans from thinking that *ReLoad* wasn't simply a remix album of *Load*. Or that simply it was just a bunch of songs that were never good enough for *Load* in the first place.

"I think a lot of people think it's just the scraps, but it's not," Ulrich countered. "I have to sit there and convince myself that I've written

ABOVE LEFT Kirk at Reading Festival, August 24, 1997.

ABOVE Kirk at one of the Bridge School Benefit shows in October 1997.

RIGHT James playing acoustically at the Bridge School Benefit, October 1997.

FAR RIGHT A nice B/W studio shot from the *ReLoad* era.

BELOW Poor Re-Touring Me, promoting *ReLoad* live 1997/1998.

27 songs that are equally good. If number 17 wasn't good enough, I'd throw it away. I believed from minute one. That's why we kept writing these fucking songs. We normally stop at 12 when we write albums, but we knew that we wanted to develop all 27 of these songs. That they were all good enough."

Did he have a point? Maybe. Preceded by a week with the new single, 'The Memory Remains', a haunting slice of Southern gothic which featured 1960s icon Marianne Faithfull. It was catchy enough as a single, and an excellent song. But there were some more fine songs to be heard on *ReLoad*, none more so than raging opener 'Fuel', which rapidly became a live and fan favourite. 'Devil's Dance' too was a raised

tempo rocker, whilst the bullish 'Better Than You' even earned the band their fourth Grammy award. One of the album's bigger surprises is the over seven minutes-long alternative ballad 'Low Man's Lyric', complete with hurdy-gurdy and touching, very personal lyrics. 'Fixxxer' too, showed the increasingly personal nature of Hetfield's lyrics (they'd been moving ever more in that direction since *Metallica*) as he railed against abuse of all kinds.

One month before the album's release the band played two semi-acoustic shows at Neil Young's Bridge School Benefit, an annual two day event to raise money for this school for children with special needs, where they debuted 'Low Man's Lyric' off the new album and played

an impressive version of 'Poor Twisted Me' off its predecessor live for the first time. Around the album's release the band played five small club shows throughout Europe to promote the album. Live tracks from the stop at London's Ministry of Sound ended up as B-sides on various singles taken off the album.

Looking back, *ReLoad* doesn't have as many really good songs as *Load*, although it still went straight in at No. 1 in the US album charts where it's sold over three million copies, so hardly a flop, even if it did raise more questions about Metallica. But in the end, it's not even their most disputed album. Oh no, you'd have to wait for their next studio effort for that!

THE 2000s

In the previous two decades of Metallica's existence the band had dealt with their fair share of trials and tribulations, but those had always been countered, or to a lesser extent papered over, with the ever burgeoning sense of achievement and ever increasing commercial success. In their third decade the band would face possibly their sternest tests outside of the tragic death of bassist Cliff Burton in 1986. Indeed, for long parts of the first decade of the new millennium, it must have felt like the band had to counter one obstacle after another.

Despite some sensing a creative wobble with 1997's *ReLoad*, Metallica ended the 1990s strongly, the impressive double covers set *Garage Inc.* and the symphonic *S&M* live album both helping re-establish some of their reputation. In 2000 the band picked up their fifth Grammy award in Best Hard Rock category for their cover of Thin Lizzy's 'Whiskey In The Jar' from *Garage Inc.* and in April the soundtrack for *Mission: Impossible II*, included a brand new Metallica song called 'I Disappear'.

However, hearing the unreleased track on the radio brought the band, particularly Ulrich, into contact with file sharing network Napster, which they duly issued with a lawsuit. Ulrich was booed at the 2000 MTV Music Video Awards, and the band became the subject of a satirical cartoon series called *Napster Bad*.

Things took a turn for the worse in January 2001 when Jason Newsted quit the band, having previously clashed with James Hetfield over his

side project Echobrain. In July, three months after the remaining trio had begun working on a follow-up to *ReLoad*, James Hetfield went into rehab, throwing the band's future into doubt. The fact that meanwhile the band won its sixth Grammy award, for Best Rock Instrumental for the *S&M* version of 'The Call Of Ktulu', offered little respite.

Much of 2002 was spent working on the new album, after Hetfield returned, with a stipulation of Hetfield's that he could only work on

the record between noon and 4pm and spend the rest of the time with his family. The entire process was filmed for a documentary called *Some Kind Of Monster*, eventually released in January 2004. Metallica announced that their new bassist was ex-Suicidal Tendencies, ex-Ozzy Osbourne man Robert Trujillo in early 2003.

St. Anger was released in June 2003, and although it went straight in at No. 1 in the US album charts, the reaction of fans and critics was poor to mixed. Arguably the worst sounding Metallica album since *...And Justice For All*, the album eschewed guitar solos and featured another diabolical drum sound. Despite this, the band picked up their seventh Grammy for the track 'St. Anger', and did what they did best – hit the road – where performances were hailed as a triumph. The band toured *St. Anger* for two years, and spent much of 2005 off the road except for two hometown shows opening for The Rolling Stones.

In spring 2006 the band's website announced that they would not be working with Bob Rock, producer of their last four studio albums. Instead Rick Rubin, who had previously worked with The Cult, Red Hot Chili Peppers and AC/DC would be the band's forthcoming producer. During the summer the band once again escaped from the studio and played a series of live shows in Europe, South Africa, Japan and South Korea where the entire *Master of Puppets* album was played live, celebrating it's 25th anniversary. Finally in December 2006 they released the DVD *The Videos – 1989–2004*, a collection of promo videos.

The band and Rubin entered Sound City studios in Los Angeles in April 2007 to start the recording of the new album that ran on for over a year, ending in May 2008. *Death Magnetic* was released that September, and again hit the top spot in the US charts, making Metallica the first band to have five such consecutive studio albums. It also hit No. 1 in 32 other countries, including the UK. The album garnered some of the best reviews the band had received for over a decade. In the live arena Metallica remained nigh on untouchable, and again the ensuing tour in support of *Death Magnetic* drew rave reviews. Another career high was reached in April 2009 when it was announced that Metallica would be inducted into the Rock And Roll Hall of Fame. Cliff Burton's father Ray Burton accepted the induction on behalf of his late son.

In 2010 Metallica began a series of concerts with the so-called Big Four of thrash, hitting the European touring circuit with, amongst others, Slayer, Megadeth and Anthrax in tow. Although 2011 was supposed to be a quiet year for the band they did bring the Big Four to the US for the first time in April of that year, then headed off to Europe in July for five more Big Four gigs, including one at Knebworth in the

OPPOSITE LEFT With System Of A Down at the *Kerrang!* Awards in August 2003.

OPPOSITE RIGHT Hell yeah! Hetfield doing what he does best.

ABOVE RIGHT Doing their best Led Zeppelin imitation for *Esquire* magazine, New York City, July 8, 2003.

RIGHT Back after the break. On tour again in the early 2000s.

UK, as well as shows in Germany, Italy, France and Sweden. There was also one further Big Four show in the US in September, at New York's famous Yankee Stadium.

These concerts have continued around the world, the quartet first appearing together on UK soil at the Sonisphere festival in 2011. And despite having commented to the press about what might happen with their next studio album, in June 2011, Metallica announced they would be recording an album with rock veteran Lou Reed. The resultant album, *Lulu*, saw the light of day in October of that year, although the response was far from good.

Metallica celebrated their 30th anniversary in San Francisco in December 2011 with four shows at The Fillmore. Tickets to the shows were only available to members of the official fan club. The shows were a Metallica fan's dream come true with a completely different setlist each night that contained a mix of classics, hits, rarely played songs, songs never played live before and even a completely new song. The many guests that joined the band on stage at the shows included ex-band members Dave Mustaine, Ron McGovney and Jason Newsted, and even as far back as Hugh Tanner and Lloyd Grant, and a selection of heavy metal celebrities including Rob Halford, John Bush, Glenn Danzig, Ozzy Osbourne and Geezer Butler. Each night was hosted by Jim Breuer, the famed stand-up comedian, and also featured a nightly game show, a nightly tribute to Cliff Burton, a Metallica Museum, limited edition posters and coin giveaways via the balloon drop at the end of the night. The day after each show the new song of the previous night was available to members of the fan club on iTunes for free. A Metallica fan's dream come true indeed. A week after the shows Metallica released the four songs on an EP called *Beyond Magnetic*.

In 2012 the band announced their own festival called Orion Music + More, that took place in June 2012 in Atlantic City, New Jersey, where the band headlined performing both *Metallica* and *Ride The Lightning* on consecutive nights. Once again they also played a series of European outdoor dates where 1991's *The Black Album* was played in its entirety, albeit in reverse order, starting with 'The Struggle Within' and ending with crowd-pleaser 'Enter Sandman'. At the end of the summer the band played an unpreceded series of no less than eight shows in Mexico City, Mexico on a new, multi-million-dollar super stage to rehearse for the subsequent recording of the first 3D concert DVD ever, in Vancouver, Canada.

At the time of writing, it appears that 2013–14 was largely spent working on new material, with a view to releasing their tenth studio album in 2015. It is eagerly anticipated.

OPPOSITE Hetfield and Trujillo on their knees at the Fillmore, San Francisco, December 2011.

RIGHT Table number from the band's induction in the Rock and Roll Hall of Fame in 2009.

ST. ANGER

"We went from one extreme to the other; from hating each other to not talking to hugging and crying over every note... It was crazy – one to the other. They're both unrealistic. Somewhere in the middle is where we need to live, and balance is difficult at times, especially for myself, who likes extremes, or thinks I like them."

This is how James Hetfield recalled making *St. Anger*. To even hear such words as "hugging" and "crying" coming from the mouth of the band's stoic figurehead seem a little shocking. No longer the quiet, strong loner with an affectation for looking like a redneck, but rather the dutiful family man and earnest, hard working band member.

Today, Hetfield stands strong above the demons that plagued him back in 2001. And yet it was on a hunting trip in Siberia, when Metallica's frontman found himself drinking vodka for breakfast, he realized that crunch time had come. Three months after the band had begun work on their eighth studio album, and six months after bassist Jason Newsted quit the band, Metallica weren't just in serious trouble. Their very existence was threatened.

Having rented an old army barracks on a disused army base and now park in San Francisco (the Presidio), work with producer Bob Rock (already standing in for the errant Newsted on bass) ground to a halt entirely as the band sat around waiting to learn if Hetfield might ever return to the fold. When he eventually did after nine months, it was under the condition that he could only work with the band between twelve noon and four in the afternoon, spending the rest of the time with his family. Given that the entire period was under scrutiny from a film crew (all revealed in the 2004 movie *Some Kind Of Monster*) it was not what you'd call the ideal backdrop to record such an important album for the band.

Metallica themselves were already under pressure to deliver something special, given the less then celebratory reaction to both *Load* and *ReLoad*. Even if chart positions and sales figures intimated that all was well, the gulf between the band and their fanbase was ever growing. The band may have steadied the flow of discontent towards the end of the 1990s with sterling live shows and the well received covers album *Garage Inc.*, and they were still a Grammy shoe-in. But as the once close-knit ensemble unravelled before their very eyes, Metallica seemed unsure of where to go with their new record.

What Metallica did do, perhaps with one eye on their past and one ear in the direction of those who never wanted the band to change in the first place, was not seek to expand their sound as they clearly had done

ABOVE Despite a new album the band found some time to sit back and relax.

OPPOSITE ABOVE All dressed up for *MTV Icon*, May 3, 2003.

OPPOSITE BELOW Live Anger.

OVERLEAF *St. Anger* hits the streets in June 2003.

with *Load* and *ReLoad*, but attempt to recapture the spirit that had made them special in the first place. But such a move often smacks of desperation. Of a band having lost itself and trying desperately seeking some kind of salvation.

One thing Metallica did agree on was that they use the turmoil and angst they were going through to some effect musically (something they would relay in the album's title), and yet the one thing they perhaps needed more than anything was the spirit that had held the band together over two decades, during which time they had endured enough setbacks and hardship to fell many bands. But Metallica recorded *St. Anger* devoid of that spirit. They initially wrote more songs than they'd be able to fit on the album and had to choose which ones to record and include on the album. Each band member made a shortlist of songs to include, and as it turned out the four that were on everyone's list were the four most vitriolic ones they had written and formed the blueprint for what *St. Anger* became: a bubbling cauldron of venom, bile and retribution.

Released on June 5, 2003, *St. Anger*, perhaps predictably, shot to the top of the charts in the US and 30 other countries. It has since sold around six million copies worldwide. But the initial reaction was mixed.

"It was the fact that there were no real songs on there," producer Bob Rock would later explain. "That was because the guy who writes the songs couldn't do it, because of where he was personally. So what *St. Anger* became was what the band could do at that point and it is exactly that. It was riffs strung together."

For a band so adept at penning memorable material, even if it was aggressive, some of the material on *St. Anger* is poor. There is little memorable on offer. The absence of any guitar solos was immediately picked up on, as was the appalling drum sound (Ulrich opted to record without his snare drum on). Making no bones about it, *St. Anger* is the worst sounding Metallica album ever. *...And Justice For All* might not have sounded great, but at least it had a lot of great songs to elevate it. A new recording of the album with a decent drum sound and ditto production might do the album justice as tracks like 'Frantic', 'Dirty Window' and the title track are not bad at all and do hold up live in concert. Even album closer 'All Within My Hands' turned out to be an amazing song when performed acoustically at 2007's Bridge School Benefit shows in Mountain View, California.

"All the work that we went through on *St. Anger*, it was said that it was not for that album, it was for the next album, and that makes total sense," Hetfield later said. "*St. Anger* was pretty much a statement – it felt like the purging of a feeling. And this record is more us working together – in harmony, in friction, in happiness, in sadness... all of that put together. And we're able to get through it – we've walked through the fire; we know how hot it can get, and we don't need to go there again."

JAMES HETFIELD

Seen by many as the figurehead of Metallica, James Hetfield has, for many years, been regarded as both an icon and a role model within the world of heavy metal. A commanding frontman on stage, Hetfield is a quiet and thoughtful – even intense – person off it yet one who has certainly known how to enjoy himself when the mood took him. It's easy to see why, when faced with competition like Axl Rose, it was Hetfield to whom the metal youth looked up to, as much for what he said, as for how he said it.

Born James Alan Hetfield on August 3, 1963 in Downey, California, Hetfield's early life was as intense as he himself can sometimes appear. What is also clear is that his early years have had a huge influence in shaping both the man and his music. Both of Hetfield's parents were strict followers of the Christian Science faith (not to be confused with the headline-grabbing Scientology) which rejects the use of medicines for curing ailments, whilst also believing that the power of prayer can heal. This latter factor would wield huge influence over the young Hetfield, whose mother Cynthia, a light opera singer, died of cancer when he was young. His father Virgil, a truck driver, would also succumb to the disease. The effect on James must have been immense, and has since surfaced in lyrics to songs like 'The God That Failed', 'Until It Sleeps' and the evocative ballad from *Load*, 'Mama Said'.

Hetfield's first musical forays were when he began piano lessons, aged nine. He later progressed to playing on his older brother's drum kit before finally picking up a guitar when he was 14. James' first band was called Obsession and his early musical influences ranged from Aerosmith, Black Sabbath and Led Zeppelin to Queen and The Beatles. Hetfield sang lead vocals for Obsession, and it was during his time with the band that he met Ron McGovney, who originally acted as a roadie and later became a member of the band himself.

RIGHT James Hetfield, rhythm guitar!

OPPOSITE James inspects Oakland Stadium, the day before the Day On The Green. October 1991.

LEFT James playing his beloved Iron Cross signature ESP.

OPPOSITE James live on tour for *The Black Album* in 1992.

Phantom Lord was Hetfield's next group, by which time he was singing and playing guitar before once again hooking up with Ron McGovney, living in a house owned by McGovney's parents. The pair then formed Leather Charm, with Hetfield on vocals alone and McGovney on bass. As the band disintegrated and Hetfield was looking for a new drummer, ex-Leather Charm guitarist Hugh Tanner introduced him to Lars Ulrich.

Having formed Metallica with Ulrich, Hetfield was initially reluctant to take on the lead vocalist role and at one point future Armored Saint and Anthrax vocalist John Bush was considered for the role. When Dave Mustaine was drafted in as guitarist the band even toyed with the idea of Mustaine as sole guitar player. However Mustaine's time in the band was fractious to say the least, and eventually Kirk Hammett of Exodus was drafted in with Hetfield on dual role as guitar player and singer.

Both Hetfield's character and talent as a musician developed tenfold as Metallica's career advanced, and the man singing on *Ride The Lightning* bears little resemblance to the relative boy who performed on *Kill 'Em All*. However his character took a huge body blow on September 27, 1986, when much-loved Metallica bassist Cliff Burton was killed as Metallica's tour bus skidded off the road, turning over on a patch of black ice near Ljungby in Sweden, throwing the sleeping Burton out of a window. Rumour suggests that Burton was sleeping in what was actually Hetfield's bunk at the time, and if true, the effect on Hetfield must have been immense. This horrific incident might go some way to explaining why Burton's replacement, Jason Newsted, never seemed completely welcomed into Metallica, and why Hetfield allegedly wears Burton's skull ring on his right hand.

A further incident occurred at a gig with Guns N' Roses at Montreal's Olympic Stadium in August 1992, when Hetfield accidentally strayed into part of the band's immense pyrotechnic display. Although his guitar shielded much of the blast, his left side suffered second and third degree burns. He made a swift recovery however, and was back on stage in a mere 17 days.

During the recording of *St. Anger* James Hetfield was forced to enter rehab for alcoholism and obsessive-compulsive disorder. He spent up to two months in rehab and a further seven with his family (he married his wife Francesca in 1997, and the couple have three children), before returning to action with Metallica. The entire uncomfortable period was highlighted in the 2004 documentary film *Some Kind Of Monster*.

Hetfield has remained sober ever since, and has toured the world consistently with Metallica, recording the studio albums *Death Magnetic* in 2008 and *Lulu* with Lou Reed in 2011. And his role as commander-in-chief remains untouched.

DEATH MAGNETIC

On March 14, 2007, Metallica's official website issued a statement: "Metallica left the comfort of HQ this week to descend upon the greater Los Angeles area to begin recording their ninth original album." Had you asked any Metallica fan at that point what they really wanted to hear from the band, the chances are you'd have got the flippant remark, "Anything but *St. Anger!*".

But if you'd have pushed them, then they'd most likely have mumbled something along the lines of "...maybe *Master of Puppets* crossed with *Metallica*..." To a certain extent, with *Death Magnetic*, that's exactly what Metallica fans got.

The band's last two studio offerings, 1997's *ReLoad* and 2003's *St. Anger*, had certainly seen the Kings of Metal's crown slip somewhat, even if Metallica were still considered a massive live draw, and sales still held up against increasingly thin opposition. But no matter how off the rails the band seemed to have gone, one sensed that the desire to get things right, to reclaim ground they once so easily regarded as their own, still burned bright within the band.

The signs were good. *St. Anger* might have been a stinker of a record

sonically and a misguided attempt to recapture the brute force of their early records, but it at least displayed a sense of some apparent understanding that things might have gone awry. Even if the end result flattered to deceive (at the very least), the very fact the band were acknowledging the need to move onwards in the right direction was better than blindly refusing to acknowledge any of the mounting concerns.

The guiding light for *Death Magnetic* would arrive in the form of chosen producer Rick Rubin. Initial writing for the new album began as far back as 2004, if what the band were then saying in radio interviews is true. However they did not enter Sound City studios in Los Angeles until April 2007, so there was plenty of time to mull over how the new music was going to sound.

Rubin, whose hand had guided the Red Hot Chili Peppers and Johnny Cash to such commercial heights, might not have seemed an obvious choice. However Rubin's advice to Metallica – to think back to their early days – and imagine themselves back in 1985, living at the Metallica mansion, with no money, hungry for success. Rubin, it appears, was spot on.

Metallica thrived under Rubin's tutelage. In May 2006, the band updated their website with a new video message letting fans in on the

band's progress – in itself a sign of the emerging confidence within the Metallica camp.

"If you're in the studio, everybody presumes you're recording or making a record. Last time there was no real separation between the writing process and the recording process," announced Lars. "With *St. Anger* nobody brought in any pre-recorded stuff or ideas; it was just make it up on the spot, be in the moment. So this time we are doing exactly what we did on all the other albums: first we're writing, then we're recording. The only difference is that we're writing where we record. So we're writing here at HQ because this is our home, we're writing in the studio."

Work on the new album was concluded in June 2008 at Malibu's Shangri La studios and at the band's own HQ in San Rafael in Marin County, where the album was mastered by the hand of Ted Jensen of Sterling Sound. *Death Magnetic* was wrapped up on August 10, 2008 and was released on September 12, 2008. It was mistakenly sold in France two weeks early, when an employee of Virgin's Megastore in Paris accidentally unboxed the wrong supply of CD's and placed it in the store ahead of its official release. In turn this of course saw the music appear on the Internet. But unlike the Napster furore at the start of the decade Ulrich reacted with comparative calm about the development, telling a San Francisco radio station "It's 2008 and it's part of how it is these days, so we're happy. We're fine."

The album title was, in part, inspired by the late Alice In Chain singer Layne Staley, a photo of which had been pinned to the studio wall by Kirk Hammett during recording.

"The title, to me, started out as a kind of tribute to people who have fallen in our business, like Layne Staley and a lot of people who've died," explained Hetfield. "rock and roll martyrs of sorts. And then it kind of grew from there, thinking about death... some people are drawn towards it, and just like a magnet, and other people are afraid of it and push. Also the concept that we're all gonna die sometimes is over-talked about and then a lot of times never talked about — no one wants to bring it up; it's the big white elephant in the room. But we all have to deal with it at some point."

However morbid, the album was greeted as a something of a revelation by fans. Lead single 'The Day That Never Comes' was a slice of prime catchy-but-hard-hitting Metallica, a fine tune to hit radio with. The remainder of the album packed the kind of weighty punch fans had longed for in the wake of the trebly *St. Anger*. And there were guitar solos aplenty, with only the final track 'My Apocalypse' weighing in at under six minutes. The band even felt so emboldened as to include 'The Unforgiven III' in a show of defiance after the second part of the song, from *ReLoad*, had been pilloried. ...'III' would even get nominated for a Grammy award, losing out to AC/DC's 'War Machine'!

To celebrate the release, the band played two shows to fan club members and contest winners at Berlin's O2 Arena, on the day of release, the first show ever at this brand new venue, and London's venue of the same name three days later. Around the London show the band also played an intimate Radio One show at the BBC Theatre and visited Jools Holland for a second time on his TV programme, showcasing new material for the first time.

Another massive commercial success for the band, their fifth consecutive No. 1 studio album on the US charts (the only band ever to do so), *Death Magnetic* might arguably not be Metallica's greatest album, but it certainly is a bloody good one. More than good enough to steer the band through waters that had, until it's release, become increasingly choppy. Mixing the aggression of *Master of Puppets* with the assuredness of *Metallica* – there's life in the old dogs yet!

OPPOSITE The world premiere of *Death Magnetic*. Berlin, Germany, September 12, 2008.

RIGHT Hetfield invites the crowd to sing along.

LULU (WITH LOU REED)

"It's not a 100% Metallica record. It's a recording project. Let's put it that way."

That was how Metallica guitarist Kirk Hammett somewhat cryptically told *Noisecreep* in February 2011 what the band were up to when news broke that the metal titans were back working on a new record. Well, 'project' was certainly one way of describing the resulting *Lulu* album.

The seeds for this seemingly unlikely project were sewn when Metallica and Lou Reed met at the 25th anniversary shows for the Rock and Roll Hall of Fame at New York's Madison Square Garden over the weekend of October 29 and 30, 2009. Both inductees of the Rock and Roll Hall of Fame, on April 4, 2009 they played 'White Light/White Heat' and 'Sweet Jane' (a classic Reed-penned Velvet Underground track) together at the show. Plans were laid down to get together and record some material. The original idea was that Metallica re-record some material that Reed had left unreleased. That might have been more palatable for Metallica fans, but the end result proved entirely different.

At some point in proceedings, Reed presented Metallica with some demos which formed the basis of music for a theatre production called *Lulu*, which was based on two turn-of the-century plays which had inspired a 1929 silent movie *Pandora's Box* and the 1930s opera *Lulu*.

Whether Reed, who had previously been touring with art/jazz/metal noise merchants Metal Machine Trio, recalling his near incomprehensible 1975 album *Metal Machine Music*, felt that it was Metallica who could bring to life the then stilted work, cunningly engineered the whole scenario, we shall never know. Certainly, for most of Metallica's audience, such overt posturing was not what they wanted from Metallica. Having endured the image change in the mid-90s, and the near-meltdown of their heroes at the turn of the century, only to see Metallica largely resurrect themselves with *Death Magnetic*, *Lulu* was hardly going to be welcomed.

The album was recorded at HQ studios in San Rafael in California between April and June 2011. And yet it was only after the entire thing had been recorded that the announcement was made that the next Metallica release would be a collaboration with Lou Reed.

One of the first people to hear any of the new material was *Rolling Stone's* David Fricke. Having heard the tracks 'Pumping Blood' and 'Mistress Dread', he described the combination of Reed and Metallica as "a raging union of Reed's 1973 noir classic *Berlin* and Metallica's 86 crusher *Master of Puppets*". Surely anything that drew parallels with Metallica's magnum opus had to be worth something to their ever-clamouring hardcore fanbase, didn't it? The reality suggested something entirely different...

LEFT Metallica and Lou Reed promoting the *Lulu* album in Europe, November 2011.

RIGHT White Light, White Heat: "Loutallica" live in Milan, Italy, November 13, 2011.

The track 'The View' was streamed online, attracting twice as many dislikes as likes from fans. When the album reviews rolled in, by and large, worse was to come. Noted UK website *The Quietus* suggested the album had "the effect of Lou Reed ranting over some Metallica demos that were never intended for human consumption", while noted pop culture writer Chuck Klostermann stated "if the Red Hot Chili Peppers acoustically covered the 12 worst Primus songs for Starbucks it would still be (slightly) better than this." Not everyone was so appalled however. Avant-garde UK music publication *The Wire* found the album favourable, but then one suspects they may have done so with the full knowledge of how annoyed it would make Metallica's own fans. *Uncut* gave it a positive review as well, praising it as "the most extraordinary, passionate and just plain brilliant record either participant has made for a long while".

The band themselves were swift to condemn the detractors. Hetfield sarcastically slated what he called "fearful people typing from their mom's basement they still live in" while Lars Ulrich referred back to a longstanding favoured argument of his, saying "in 1984 when hardcore Metallica fans heard acoustic guitars on 'Fade To Black' there was a nuclear meltdown in the metal community". And Lou Reed? He just grumbled "I don't have any fans left. After *Metal Machine Music* they all fled. Who cares?"

Maybe Lou Reed really didn't care. After all, he had nothing to lose, teaming up with the raging metallic wall of noise Metallica did, in all actuality, supply to his bile-filled poetic ranting that forms the bedrock of *Lulu*. It was hardly going to do his cause any harm, was it? For Metallica though, having just appeared to salvage at least three quarters of their credibility with *Death Magnetic*, surely such a left-field turn was quite a risk to take. Even as an act of defiance, they were hardly in a position to be thumbing their noses at their fanbase.

So is *Lulu* the disaster that some reviewers and disappointed fans make it seem? No, it isn't. True, it's not a Metallica album per se, despite the fact that it still has their name emblazoned on it and they wrote all the music on it. (Reed wrote all of the lyrics) It's an avant-garde metal album. Then again, anyone who expected an album that has Lou Reed contributing to it to be easy listening hasn't really been paying attention to any of the material he's put out in his career.

To promote the album two videos were shot, for the tracks 'Iced Honey' and 'The View', both directed by Darren Aronofsky. Reed and Metallica also set out on a series of promotional performances in Europe playing tracks from the album as well as some old Velvet Underground songs. At the time Reed hinted at doing a few shows with Metallica to perform the entire album live, but if that's ever going to happen remains to be seen.

LARS ULRICH

Whatever you think of Lars – and opinions stretch from one end of the popular blanket to the very opposite – there remains one undeniable fact. Without Lars Ulrich, there would certainly be no Metallica.

He may not be the most technically gifted drummer and he may have a mouth that's tempted to shift into overdrive. He may have a fondness for 1990s UK indie bands and a passion for art at odds with both his fanbase and his very roots. Oh, and allegedly, he also once threw up over Lemmy's cowboy boots! Yet if it wasn't for the genuine passion that Ulrich displays for heavy metal, especially the NWOBHM, and his determination and drive, then you wouldn't be reading this right now.

Lars Ulrich, born in Gentofte, Denmark on December 26, 1963, was destined to follow in the footsteps of his father Torben Ulrich as a professional tennis player, until his over-riding passion for heavy metal took a hold of him.

When the family moved to America, it was intended to further young Lars' tennis career. The fact that, at aged 13, he'd been given his first drum kit (a Ludwig), wasn't just a reflection of his passion for music, but also to aid his dexterity with a view to his tennis. But by then Lars clearly had other ideas.

ABOVE Crew wristband from the Wherever We May Roam tour.

RIGHT Lars appreciates the crowd, live in East Rutherford, NJ on the Damaged Justice tour, 1989.

BELOW Lars enjoying the backstage catering. Monsters of Rock, Germany, August 1987.

OPPOSITE He bangs the drums. Lars where he belongs.

Back in 1975 Torben had been given tickets to see Deep Purple in Copenhagen, and when a friend dropped out, nine-year-old Lars went along. The concert was to change his life. A year after the Ulrich family arrived in America, an 18-year old Lars Ulrield was making his way back to Europe to follow his true obsession. Heavy metal.

By the time he returned to America, Ulrich was a man possessed. He was going to form a band and follow in the footsteps of his heroes. His first move was to place the now famous ad in *The Recycler*. This led to an initial meeting with James Hetfield. It didn't go quite as the drummer planned: "Lars had a pretty crappy drum kit with one cymbal," Hetfield recalled in *Playboy* in 2001. "It kept falling over, and we'd have to stop and he'd pick the fucking thing up. He really was not a good drummer."

Even after Hetfield bailed, Lars' persisted. He kept bothering fellow tape-trading friend and now Metal Blade label owner Brian Slagel, who eventually relented and agreed to allow his 'band' a place on his *Metal Massacre* compilation. Only one problem. Lars didn't actually have a band. But he persevered with Hetfield, who with such a carrot dangling in front of him, clambered back on board. The pair, along with a guitarist Hetfield knew, Jamaican Lloyd Grant, set about recording 'Hit The Lights'.

Since their formation in 1981, both Metallica and Lars Ulrich have hit incredible highs and some murky lows. His challenge to the file-sharing website Napster, which ended up in court and with Ulrich being mercilessly parodied on the TV show *South Park* and on numerous internet sites, may have gone some way to alerting the record industry to the threat of internet piracy and illegal downloading, but it brought with it an enormous backlash from music fans, including many Metallica fans, that did the band's reputation no good.

If Hetfield is perceived, by many fans at least, as the figurehead, not least because in him they like to see something of themselves, then there is no denying that Lars is the brains. What Mick Jagger is to the Stones, Ulrich is to Metallica; the driving force, the one in control, making the main business decisions. Unlike many drummers, Ulrich is highly articulate and regarded as a good interviewee by the many journalists who have conducted interviews with him. He may not have come out of *Some Kind of Monster* with his reputation glowing, and even when he pushes Metallica into new musical challenges that go against the grain of some of the band's fans, one suspects that while it is easy to lay claim to his ego running out of control, he actually does it with the band's best interests at heart.

One only has to look at the fact that, when he discovered that heavyweight management Q Prime were interested in the band, he sought out Peter Mensch's phone number and telephoned him from a public call box to set further wheels in motion for the band, is perhaps all you need to know about the fires that continue to burn bright within Ulrich. Oasis guitarist Noel Gallagher, of whom Ulrich remains an unashamed fan may have said "He's a strange character. A strange, strange man." But the fact remains: no Ulrich – no Metallica!

FORMER BAND MEMBERS

LLOYD GRANT

Never a real member of the band, but as Lloyd Grant did appear on Metallica's very first recording we will give him the benefit of the doubt and include him in this chapter anyway. He appeared alongside Lars Ulrich and James Hetfield as part of the primordial Metallica lineup that recorded 'Hit The Lights' for Brian Slagel's *Metal Massacre* compilation. When the song was recorded, Metallica did not really exist, Ulrich having cajoled Slagel into giving his band a place on the compilation, despite the fact there wasn't actually a band! However, there's no denying that 'Hit The Lights' was the song that set forth the chain of reaction that has ultimately brought us to this very day. For the record, Ulrich played drums, Hetfield sang, played lead guitar and bass whilst Grant played the solos. When Metallica finally got up and running, Grant did not feature in the initial lineup, with Dave Mustaine taking his place. Grant later played in a band called Defcon, who released a well received demo in 1985. Little was heard in the mainstream media of Grant since then, but in an interview with *Music Legends* in November 2011 he recalled his time with Metallica, and stated that he is currently a working musician living in Canada. During the last of Metallica's four 30th anniversary shows at The Fillmore in San Francisco he played 'Hit The Lights' (as well as 'Seek & Destroy') with the band.

RON MCGOVNEY

Ron McGovney was Metallica's original bass player, performing with the band for the first 15 months of their career, before Cliff Burton replaced him.

McGovney had been a childhood friend of James Hetfield, the pair bonding over their shared love of heavy metal. Hetfield, a budding guitarist, inspired McGovney to take up bass, even offering his friend lessons. When Hetfield's previous band Phantom Lord ground to a halt, it seemed only natural the pair hook up in a new band, Leather Charm, which also featured Phantom Lord guitarist Hugh Tanner. It was out of the ashes of Leather Charm that Metallica arose, with Tanner taking his leave, replaced initially by Lloyd Grant and eventually Dave Mustaine, and Lars Ulrich on drums.

Metallica recorded a couple of demos with McGovney in the lineup, including the legendary *No Life 'Til Leather* demo, and future Metallica classics such as 'Seek And Destroy' and 'The Four Horsemen' began to take shape with him in the band. He played his last gig with Metallica

on November 30, 1982 at San Francisco's Mabuhay Gardens. He resurfaced in the 1980s with a band called Phantasm, and is today a happily married family man. Like Lloyd Grant he did appear with the band at the 30th anniversary shows in San Francisco, performing 'Hit The Lights' and 'Seek & Destroy'.

SAMMY DIJON / BRAD PARKER / JEFF WARNER

During the very early stages when Metallica was still experimenting with its lineup the band had a few very short-lived band members. Singer Sammy Dijon joined the band in March 1982, when Hetfield had decided he wanted to concentrate on playing guitar. Dijon, previously a member of local band Ruthless, rehearsed with Metallica over a three-week period but never performed a live show with the band. When it was apparent it was not working, Hetfield returned to the microphone. Guitarist Brad Parker (stage name: Damian C. Philips) played exactly one show with the band, on April 23, 1982 at The Concert Factory in Costa Mesa, California after which they decided James was going to sing and play guitar and continued as a four piece without Parker. Jeff Warner was also part of an early lineup for a very short time before the real first lineup of Ulrich, Hetfield, McGovney and Mustaine hit it off.

RIGHT Mustaine, Hetfield and McGovney giving it their best axe work at the Old Waldorf in San Francisco, November 29, 1982.

OPPOSITE Reunited at last. Dave Mustaine and James Hetfield playing together with Metallica at The Fillmore, San Francisco, December 10, 2011.

DAVE MUSTAINE

Of all the band members who passed through the ranks of Metallica, none have had as much impact on the world of metal as Dave Mustaine. Troubled yet talented, contentious yet comedic, Mustaine remains one of heavy metal's enigmas who has channelled much of the bitter, negative energy of being kicked out of the band into becoming one of Metallica's main contenders in the metal world with Megadeth.

Born in La Mesa, California on September 13, 1961, David Scott Mustaine was always something of a rebel. A youthful love of heavy metal drew him to the guitar and Mustaine joined local band Panic, but trouble swiftly reared its head when the band's guitarist and sound engineer were killed in a road accident after their first gig. Fortunately, Metallica came calling.

Mustaine's time in Metallica was equal parts triumph and tragedy. On the one hand, he was musically talented and seemed to even lead the band on that front – just lend an ear to 'The Mechanix' from the *No Life 'Til Leather* demo to hear his evident songwriting talent – while his technically expert guitar playing helped mould the early Metallica sound. Metallica parted company with Mustaine as they travelled to the East Coast to record their debut album. It was April 11, 1983. His last show with the band was at the infamous L' Amour in Brooklyn, New York two days before his (former) band mates put him on a Greyhound bus back to California.

Mustaine formed Megadeth in late 1983 and, despite a career that, in typical Mustaine fashion, has been dogged by all manner of controversy, equally hit enormous commercial heights. And despite a fractious relationship with his old band mates, the relationship between Mustaine and Metallica seems to have strengthened in the past few years, with him joining the band on stage at the aforementioned 30th anniversary shows as well as playing several shows opening for Metallica as part of the Big Four.

JASON NEWSTED

Metallica's third bassist is also the band's longest serving so far. And while the years served by Jason Newsted were graced with some of the band's greatest triumphs, they were also tainted, to a certain extent, with the perception that he was always viewed as something of an outsider.

Born Jason Curtis Newsted on March 4, 1963 in Battle Creek Michigan, Newsted joined a band called Paradox in 1982. The band changed it's name to Dogz and then later to Flotsam And Jetsam and Newsted appeared on the band's early demos as well as their highly acclaimed 1986 debut album *Doomsday For The Deceiver*, for which he penned most of the lyrics. When the position became available he auditioned against sixty other hopefuls before getting the Metallica job on October 28, 1986.

Newsted's time in Metallica saw the band attain heights previously unachieved by many rock acts, and yet it was also tainted by rumours that he was never truly accepted into the band – he only got three writing credits during his fifteen years in Metallica. This was a fact not helped by the almost inaudible bass sound on *...And Justice For All*, or the perception that he was the butt end of many practical jokes within the band.

Newsted took his leave from Metallica on January 17, 2001, stating his departure was due to "private and personal reasons and the physical damage I have done to myself over the years while playing the music that I love". In fact it meant he could concentrate on his side project Echochain without having to worry about what others might think of it. He also joined Canadian prog metallers Voivod, has worked with Ozzy Osbourne and played on several other projects since then. In April 2009 Newsted was inducted in the Rock and Roll Hall of Fame alongside his former band mates and his replacement Robert Trujillo. He also appeared with the band on their 30th anniversary shows, receiving a hero's welcome from the fans, getting to pick two songs to play with them on each of the four nights.

RIGHT The heaviest night of your life!
March 19, 1983, The Stone, San Francisco.

METALLICA LIVE

Amazingly, for a band that is considered to be heavy metal's biggest live band for years if not decades, Metallica have never released a live album in the classic sense of metal live albums. But despite the fact that the band doesn't have it's own *No Sleep 'Til Hammersmith*, *Strangers In The Night* or *Live After Death* there's an impressive amount of live material available on various releases, most of them covered here.

BELOW James right on top of it at London's O2 Arena. March 28, 2009.

OPPOSITE James out in the pouring rain. Nowhere Else To Roam Tour, Turin, Italy, spring 1993.

CLIFF 'EM ALL (1987)

As homage to original bassist Cliff Burton, this VHS was released just over a year after the bassist's tragic death. It features much fan-shot footage of the band in their earliest days, but also included are TV interviews, songs taken from various pro shot shows, including a version of Cliff's signature bass solo shot at the band's first appearance at the Day On The Green festival in 1985. Even Dave Mustaine makes an appearance on a version of 'Whiplash' shot at The Stone in San Francisco in March 1983, Cliff's second ever gig with the band.

LIVE SHIT: BINGE & PURGE (1993)

Upon its release, *Live Shit...* contained the biggest amount of Metallica live material, cramming some nine hours of live Metallica over three CDs and two DVDs (or VHS in the original box set). The music was recorded at different shows, recordings from Mexico City were used for the CDs, while a 1989 Seattle gig from the Damaged Justice Tour and a 1992 San Diego show from the Roam Tour were used for the video. Besides the music the collection also included a replica backstage pass, a photo booklet and a logo stencil. The fact that a massive, and therefore expensive, box set like this managed to reach a sales level of 15 times Platinum RIAA certification proves how much the band's fan base was waiting for the band to finally release more live material.

CUNNING STUNTS (1998)

A two-disc DVD of two concerts at Tarrant County Center, Fort Worth in Texas from May 9–10, 1997, directed by Wayne Isham. A rare Metallica performance that did not use Ennio Morricone's 'Ecstasy of Gold', opening with the Bad Seed Jam segueing into a cover of the Anti Nowhere League's 'So What'. Notable at the time for having three tracks using multiple-angle camera shots. The pyro scene during 'Enter Sandman' is particularly impressive. Features great images of the show

S&M (1999)

Both a CD and a film version of the band's concerts recorded with the Michael Kamen conducted San Francisco Symphony Orchestra at the Berkeley Community Theater in April 1999. The project was inspired by Cliff Burton's love of classical music, and the 1969 Deep Purple album *Concerto for Group and Orchestra* of which the band were fans. Two new songs were recorded especially for the album, 'No Leaf Clover' and '- Human'. Singles for 'No Leaf Clover' and the S&M version of 'Nothing Else Matters' did very well on the charts.

ORGULLO, PASION Y GLORIA: TRES NOCHES EN LA CIUDAD DE MEXICO (2009)

The title translates into English as Pride, Passion & Glory: Three Nights In Mexico, this was a hefty live set that was originally released in Latin America only. Recorded at three different shows at Foro Sol in Mexico City on June 4, 6 and 7, 2009 on the band's lengthy World Magnetic trek, it was released as a 19-track DVD, a Blu-ray version of the DVD, a digi-pack featuring DVD and two CDs and a deluxe version with two DVD and two CDs. This is the first release to feature live material of the *Death Magnetic* album.

FRANÇAIS POUR UN NUIT (2009)

A French-only release, this set was recorded on the World Magnetic Tour at one of the most spectaculair venues the band has ever played, the Arena of Nîmes in France on July 7, 2009. Initially it's only been released as a special edition box set that featured the DVD, a copy of *Death Magnetic* on CD, a t-shirt, a laminated pass and five special photos by long time band collaborator Ross Halfin. Later on also a regular DVD and a Blu-ray appeared, that did not have any of the extras.

THE BIG 4: LIVE FROM SOFIA, BULGARIA (2010)

On June 22, 2010, Metallica, Slayer, Megadeth and Anthrax – the so-called big four of thrash metal, appeared together on the same stage at the Bulgarian stop of the travelling Sonisphere festival, at the Vasil Levski National stadium in Sofia. On the night the four bands were filmed and the whole event was released on a regular DVD as well as on Blu-ray. A box set with the DVD as well as all music on five CDs was available as a limited edition. On the night the entire show was transmitted via satellite to 800 cinemas worldwide, making it one of the biggest events of its kind ever.

SIX FEET DOWN UNDER (2010)

An Australian and New Zealand-only release to promote their 2010 Antipodean tour, this eight-track live EP is something of an anomaly that harks back to *Cliff 'Em All*, in as much as it featured a mix of fan-recorded and band archive material taken from the four

years that Metallica had toured down under; 1989, 1993, 1998 and 2004.

LIVE AT GRIMEY'S (2010)

On June 12, 2008, the day before they appeared at the Bonnarroo Music Festival, Metallica performed a set at The Basement, a small venue in the basement of Grimey's New And Pre-Loved Music Store, in Nashville, Tennessee. The nine-track EP was released on CD and vinyl and sold only through independent record stores and the band's website. It is the first Metallica release to feature the band's original logo for over a decade.

QUEBEC MAGNETIC (2012)

This 26-track live DVD, directed by Wayne Isham and recorded in Quebec on the band's World Magnetic Tour. Fanclub members got to vote which of the two nights that were filmed would be used as the

DVD's main feature and the bonus tracks were the songs only played on the other night. Three Metallica songs on this set had never appeared on film before; 'The End Of The Line', 'My Apocalypse' and 'The Judas Kiss'.

PEACE, LOVE AND METAL (2014)

This 16 song live album, including new song 'Lords of Summer' (due for inclusion on the new album in 2015) comprises the band's Glastonbury Festival set in front of a 100,000-strong crowd on the famous Worthy Farm. Despite the negativity that surrounded the band as headline act, the band couldn't care less – they nailed it and won over the crowd.

ABOVE *Master of Puppets* live in Vancouver, Canada, August 2012.

OPPOSITE Done Roaming! The last show of the Roam tour, Werchter, Belgium, July 4, 1993.

METALOGRAPHY

In September 2013 Metallica released *Through The Never*, a concert film unlike any that has been seen before. The film splices together the surreal misadventures of a young man called Trip intercut with spectacular gig footage the band recorded a year earlier. Between the release of this movie and Metallica's first demo, the *Whiskey Audition Tape* of March 1982, over thirty years of metal history was created and performed. The following demos, singles, studio albums and concert films are the choice cuts of Metallica's rise from San-Fran metal fans to, undoubtedly, the world's biggest ever heavy metal band.

EARLY DEMOS
Whiskey Audition Tape (recorded at Whiskey a Go Go, LA), March 1982
Ron McGovney's '82 Garage Demo, March 1982
No Life 'Til Leather, July 1982
Metal Up Your Ass, November 1982
Megaforce demo, March 1983

EPS
The $5.98 E.P.: Garage Days Re-Revisited, August 1997
Six Feet Down Under, September 2010
Six Feet Down Under II, November 2010
Live at Grimey's, November 2010
Beyond Magnetic, December 2011

SINGLES
'Whiplash', 1983
'Jump in the Fire', 1984
'Creeping Death', 1984
'Master of Puppets', 1986
'Harvester of Sorrow', 1988
'Eye of the Beholder', 1988
'One', 1989
'Enter Sandman', 1991
'The Unforgiven', 1991
'Nothing Else Matters', 1992
'Wherever I May Roam', 1992
'Sad But True', 1993
'Until It Sleeps', 1996

'Hero of the Day', 1996
'Mama Said', 1996
'King Nothing', 1997
'The Memory Remains', 1997
'The Unforgiven II', 1998
'Fuel', 1998
'Turn the Page', 1998
'Whiskey in the Jar', 1999
'Die, Die My Darling', 1999
'Nothing Else Matters '99', 1999
'No Leaf Clover', 1999
'I Disappear', 2000
'St. Anger', 2003
'Frantic', 2003
'The Unnamed Feeling', 2004
'Some Kind of Monster', 2004
'The Day That Never Comes', 2008
'My Apocalypse', 2008
'Cyanide', 2008
'The Judas Kiss', 2008
'All Nightmare Long', 2008
'Broken, Beat and Scarred', 2009
'The View' (with Lou Reed), 2011

COMPILATION ALBUMS
Garage Inc., November 1998

STUDIO ALBUMS
Kill 'Em All, July 1983
Ride the Lightning, July 1984
Master of Puppets, March 1986

...And Justice For All, August 1988
Metallica, August 1991
Load, June 1996
ReLoad, November 1997
St. Anger, June 2003
Death Magnetic, September 2008

SOUNDTRACK ALBUMS
Metallica Through The Never, September 2013

DOCUMENTARY
Some Kind of Monster, January 2004

BOX SETS
The Good, the Bad and the Live, May 1990
Limited Edition Vinyl Box Set, November 2004
Coffin Box, 2008
The Metallica Collection, April 2009

VIDEOS & DVDS
Cliff 'Em All, 1987
2 of One, 1989
A Year And A Half In the Life of Metallica, 1992
The Videos 1989-2004, 2006

> "THE GREAT THING ABOUT OUR MUSIC IS THAT IT'S REALLY, REALLY FUN TO PLAY." *James*

OPPOSITE Live at the Monsters of Rock festival in Pforzheim, Germany. August 30, 1987.

METALLICA BOOTLEGS

The sale and purchase of unauthorized (bootleg) recordings is illegal, so we do not condone you going out and buying this type of thing, although it is a significant part of heavy metal culture. That said, there are a number of unauthorized but very interesting, good quality recordings of Metallica through the years, a few of which are listed below.

FUCKING NUTS [11/2/1984, 2LP]

This rare double LP is one of the oldest Metallica bootlegs out there. It features Metallica's infamous show at the Aardschok Dag festival in Zwolle, Netherlands in early 1984. It was their biggest show to date for 6,500 raging Dutch headbangers, opening for Venom. What makes this bootleg especially interesting is the inclusion of a very early Dave Mustaine interview recorded just after he got kicked out of the band.

FIRST UK GIG [27/3/1984, CD]

Metallica were supposed to be touring the UK in early 1984 with The Rods and Exciter on the Hell On Earth Tour. Once the entire tour was cancelled due to poor ticket sales the band's UK label Music For Nations sprang into action and sorted out two gigs for Metallica at London's prestigious Marquee. This recording captures the first of the two, the band's first UK gig ever. It captures the youthful aggression and energy of the band in full swing.

ACTING LIKE A MANIAC [17/08/85, LP]

A recording of Metallica's first ever appearance at Donington's Monsters of Rock festival, the scene of the legendary thrashers vs. hair metal kids. With Bon Jovi also on the bill, James Hetfield wastes no time in bellowing to the crowd "If you came here to see spandex and fucking eye make-up and all that shit. And the words 'Rock 'n' roll baby' in every fucking song, this ain't the fucking band! We came here to bash some fucking heads for 50 minutes. Are you fucking with us?" It appears most of the crowd were as Metallica delivered an excellent performance. Bon Jovi got their own back two years later, buzzing Metallica with their helicopter!

THE FINAL GIG [26/09/86, 2LP]

There are better recordings from the band's Damage Inc. Tour, but none carry the relevance of this show. Why? Take a look at the date. It's the night that Cliff Burton died. A soundboard recording has long done the rounds of a stunning show that captured the classic incarnation of Metallica at their very peak. Cliff's bass solo stands out as something special. Proof if you ever needed it that in 1986 Metallica were a true force to be reckoned with, this is an emotional *tour de force*.

BEYOND THE WALLS OF SOUND [02/08/1987, CD]

Also known as Zwolle, this must rate as one of the finest bootlegs of the early Jason Newsted era band. The recording is taken from the band's appearance at that year's Aardschok Dag festival in the Netherlands, and is a direct-from-soundboard recording. Notable also for the band bringing fellow bill-members Laaz Rockit, Anthrax and Metal Church on for the final encore of 'Blitzkrieg'.

STONE COLD CRAZY [25/10/1992, 3CD]

An amazing 3CD set that captures the complete show Metallica gave at London's Wembley Arena during the Wherever We May Roam Tour. Excellent sound quality including the pre show banter as well as an interview afterwards. One of the best bootlegs to grasp the live shows of the band where in this period.

MIDDLE SHIT [17/06/1994, 2CD]

This rare 2CD from Japan is one of the finest to present a show from the 1994 summer tour. It features rare treats like 'The God That Failed', 'Disposable Heroes' and the 'Kill'/'Ride' medley, that combines tracks from the first two albums, premiered during this tour.

PREPARE FOR BATTLE [23/08/1995, 2CD]

Three days before headlining Donington in 1995 the band played a show at London's Astoria 2 to members of their fanclub. Sound quality is a bit rough, but the band premiered two new tracks, one of which would end up on *Load*, the other on *ReLoad*. The relaxed vibe and jokes in between songs make it worth checking out.

LOADING BARCELONA [23/09/1996, 2CD]

The concert featured on this 2CD is not all that rare or especially interesting, but what makes this stand out is the inclusion of the world premiere of 'Hero Of The Day'. Before the actual show started the band came out to play the song to tape a live video for it, as it was to be released as a single soon afterwards. It would be another half year before it became a regular in the setlist and hasn't been played all that often. (And not at all since 1999!)

OSLO OVERLOAD [23/11/1996, 2CD]

Though there are many Metallica CD bootlegs with recordings of their 1996 European tour, this one could very well be the best sounding one of them all. A Norwegian radio station recorded the show and broadcasted it, giving the recordings a really good, heavy thundering sound that makes this an absolute pleasure to listen to.

WOODSTOCK '99 [24/07/1999, 2CD]

Metallica headlined the East Stage on the third day of the event, coming on after a barnstorming set from the then very hip Rage Against The Machine. Undeterred, Metallica got straight down to business, ripping into 'So What', 'Master of Puppets' and 'For Whom The Bell Tolls' and continuing to deliver a killer set, concluding with a forebodingly awesome 'Battery'.

MADLY IN ANGER WITH ANTWERP [17/12/2003]

Having witnessed the adverse reaction to *St. Anger*, which was released approximately six months prior to this concert, Metallica reacted by really going for things on the road, mixing their set lists up as much as possible as if in an attempt to placate fans always hankering for the band's early raw sound. With the likes of 'Blackened', 'Harvester of Sorrow', 'Motorbreath' and 'Damage Inc.' all featuring, this gig from Antwerp, Belgium, the band were certainly bringing some classics back from the vaults. Notable for being one of the rare audience recorded bootlegs in this section, but so well recorded it almost makes you feel like you're at the gig.

BBC RADIO THEATRE [14/9/2008]

Limited to a mere 500 copies upon its release, *BBC Radio Theatre* (also known as *Live At The BBC Radio Theatre*) was one of the first Metallica bootlegs to feature material from the just-unreleased *Death Magnetic*. On top of that, it is a professional recording by the BBC, running at a full 70 minutes, and taken from the theatre inside Broadcasting House, a venue that has played host to many a famous recording and performing artist over the years. One of the best sounding bootlegs to feature the modern day lineup.

Weds. April 14, 2010   Oslo, NOR v 2

****House Song**** **PB42**
****Ecstasy of Gold**** **PB2**
****Heartbeat**** **PB16**

LIFE   LASERS
CYANIDE **DDL**

✘ FUEL   ✘ PYRO ✘
STRAW   COFFIN MOVES
****HANG KIRK****
DAY **DDL**

WOLF
****JUDAS TAPE**** **PB27**
****4 COUNT****
JUDAS KISS

SAD **DDL**   COFFIN MOVES
****UNFORGIVEN III TAPE**** **PB29**
UNFORGIVEN III
****JUSTICE TAPE**** **PB18**
JUSTICE   COFFIN MOVES
****ONE TAPE**** **PB4**
✘ ONE   ✘ PYRO ✘
****HANG (FEEDBACK)****
PUPPETZ **KORG 5**   LASERS
****BATTERY TAPE**** **PB12**
✘ BATTERY   ✘ PYRO ✘
****DOODLE****
NOTHING
SANDMAN **KORG 4 PB6** ✘ PYRO ✘

HELPLESS
PHANTOM
****HOUSE LIGHTS ON****
SEEK

"IF YOU STOP BEING A METALLICA FAN BECAUSE I WON'T GIVE YOU MY MUSIC FOR FREE, THEN F*CK YOU. I DON'T WANT YOU TO BE A METALLICA FAN." *Lars*

The publishers would like to thank the following sources for their kind permission to reproduce the pictures in this book.

2. © Bill Hale, 3. Photoshot/Tony Mottram/Retna UK, 4-5. Getty Images/John Storey/Time & Life Pictures, 6. & 7. Getty Images/Mick Hutson/Redferns, 8-9. © Ross Halfin, 10. & 12 (left) © Bill Hale, 13. © Ross Halfin, 14. (left & right) & 15. 16. (left) © Bill Hale, 16. (right), 18. 19. © Ross Halfin, 20. (top left and centre left) © Bill Hale, 21. (right) Getty Images/Paul Cronin/Redferns, 22. (left) © Ross Halfin, 22. (right) Photoshot/Retna, 23. (left & right) © Ross Halfin, 24. 26-27. Getty Images/Finn Costello/Redferns, 28. (left & right) Photoshot/Tony Mottram/Retna UK, 29. (left & right) © Ross Halfin, 30. Getty Images/Peter Pavkis/Redferns, 31. Getty Images/Bob Berg, 32. (left & right) © Ross Halfin, 32. (left) Getty Images/Paul Natkin/WireImage, 32. (right), 34-35. 36. © Ross Halfin, 37. Getty Images/ The LIFE Picture Collection, 39. (top left) Mike Cameron/Redferns, 39. (centre left) © Ross Halfin, 39. (right) Getty Images/Paul Natkin/WireImage, 40. (left) Corbis, 40. (right) Photoshot/Levy/Dalle/Retna UK, 43. (left) Getty Images/Kevin Cummins, 43. (right) © Ross Halfin, 44. Getty Images/Mick Hutson/Redferns, 45. 46. & 47. Getty Images/John Storey/Time & Life Pictures, 48. (top & bottom) © Ross Halfin, 50. (left) Corbis/Javier Cebollada/Epa, 50. (right) Getty Images/Larry Hulst/Michael Ochs Archive, 51. (left) Getty Images/Martin Philbey/Redferns, 51. (right) Photoshot/Kevin Estrada/Retna, 52. Getty Images/Tim Mosenfelder (left) 52. (centre) Getty Images/Michel Linssen, 52. (right) Getty Images/Brian Rasic, 53. (top) © Ross Halfin, 53. (bottom) Getty Images/Michel Linssen, 54. (left) Photoshot/Jamie Reid, 54. (right) Getty Images/Tim Mosenfelder, 55. (top) Getty Images/Tim Mosenfelder, 55. (left) Getty Images/George de Sota/Redferns, 55. (right) Photoshot/Melanie Weiner/Retna UK, 56. (left) © Ross Halfin, 56. (right) Getty Images/Theo Wargo/WireImage, 57. (top) Ben Watts/Corbis Outline, 57. (bottom) Getty Images/M. Caulfield/WireImage, 58-59. Getty Images/Tim Mosenfelder, 60. Corbis/Will Blochinger, 61. (top & bottom) Getty Images/Theo Wargo/WireImage, 62-63. Getty Images/Mick Hutson/Redferns, 64. Getty Images/Scott Gries, 65. © Ross Halfin, 66. Getty Images/Paul Bergen/Redferns, 67. Getty Images/Michel Linssen/Redferns, 68. Getty Images/Lester Cohen/WireImage, 69. Getty Images/Jeff Kravitz/FilmMagic, 70. Matthijs, 71. Getty Images/Noel Vasquez, 72. Getty Images/Kevin Mazur, 73. Getty Images/Stefania D'Alessandro, 74. (left & right) © Ross Halfin, 75. © Bill Hale, 76. Photoshot/Levy/Dalle/Retna UK, 77. © Ross Halfin, 78. Matthijs, 79. & 80. © Bill Hale, 81. Rex Features/Andre Csillag, 82-83. © Bill Hale, 84. Matthijs, 85. 86 & 87. © Ross Halfin, 88-89. Contour by Getty Images/Clay Patrick McBride, 90. & 96. © Ross Halfin, 96. Matthijs

Special photography by Karl Adamson

Special thanks to Bill Hale, Ross Halfin and Dave Brolan.

Extra special thanks to Matthijs Kropff for memorabilia editing, expertise and assistance.

Every effort has been made to acknowledge correctly and contact the source and/or copyright holder of each picture and Carlton Books Limited apologises for any unintentional errors or omissions, which will be corrected in future editions of this book.

LEFT Flyer for the July 3, 1988 Monsters of Rock show in Dallas, Texas

OPPOSITE One more? The Poor Touring Me tour in support of *Load*, 1996.